MEAT-FREE
MEXICAN

THOMASINA MIERS

**PHOTOGRAPHY
BY TARA FISHER**

MEAT-FREE
MEXICAN

VIBRANT VEGETARIAN RECIPES

THOMASINA MIERS

HODDER &
STOUGHTON

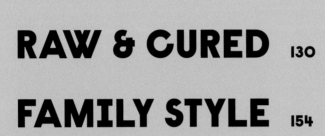

INTRODUCTION

I first went to Mexico between school and university, armed with earnings from a city job I had in London. I had no idea what to expect but took to the country as passionately as I hated the job that paid for it. Apart from the thrill of being somewhere totally foreign and astoundingly beautiful, and drinking in the exhilarating taste of freedom for the first time, it was the food that plunged me into this headlong love affair. Like many others, I had always thought that Tex-Mex was Mexico's national cuisine. But as I stomped, swam, danced and ate my way through the valleys and uplands of Oaxaca, the coast of Campeche and the Yucatán and the rainforests of Veracruz, I was astounded by the diversity of fruit and vegetables and the extraordinarily delicious food.

A myriad of wonderfully named and exotic herbs flavoured marinades and broths; an astonishing variety of chillies across the regions spiked salsas, relishes and ceviches. Wild greens, courgettes, pumpkins and mushrooms were used to fill tacos and make soups and stews; dazzlingly coloured and beautifully shaped tropical fruits I had never seen before made star appearances in *nieves* and *paletas* (sorbets and ice-lollies), fruit salads and creamy puddings. It was a far healthier and more interesting cuisine than I could ever have imagined. And it tasted amazing.

It was not until I did an event with Google, Kew and the Crop Trust years later that I learned that Mexico, along with a handful of other countries across the globe, is classified as mega-diverse.

While an island like the UK has around 2,000 different native plant species, Mexico has around 50,000 and it is the enormous range of herbs, greens, corn, chillies, squash plants, fruits and edible flowers that makes it such a special place to cook and eat.

A trip to any food market in Mexico beautifully illustrates this abundance of ingredients. Yes, there are butchers' aisles a plenty but the largest parts of the markets, and the most stunning, are piled high with mountains of carefully arranged, overlapping and beautifully patterned fruit and veg. Some of the 200 types of Mexican chillies, all with their own incredible flavours and characteristics, will be piled in various sacks and bags; heaps of corn in shades of red, dark blue, inky black, yellow or white, and bags of multi-coloured, beautifully patterned beans, will be attractively organised; radish mountains, piles of tomatoes of every colour, courgettes, pumpkins, bundles upon bundles of wild herbs, an abundance of varieties of greens and stunningly kaleidoscopic piles of exotic fruits all tempt the shopper.

Outside the markets the canny middlemen will sit, shucking corn, de-prickling cactus paddles and prepping neat packages of fresh vegetables for the shoppers to take home, an enticing version of pre-prepared veg. A love of good ingredients and cooking is written across the faces of every shopper and stall-holder; it seems to seep into every pore of Mexico's consciousness. This is a nation that culturally feels that the act of breaking bread with fellow humans is almost as important as drawing breath; where taxi drivers will converse with you at length about what their grandmother used to cook for them; where anyone you meet seems delighted to talk about where they were born and the particulars of that region's cuisine; where every occasion and event is an excuse for feasting. When I look at my own country's often ambivalent approach to good food, which is often seen as a luxury, not a necessity, I find myself wondering when and where did we get it so wrong.

When we first opened Wahaca, nearly 15 years ago, perceptions of Mexican food were understandably skewed by the meat and cheese fests in Tex-Mex restaurants across the world. Even with the explosion of 'real' Mexican restaurants opening in the UK, across Europe and as far as Australia in the last decade, there still lingers belief that Mexican food is mainly meat heavy and unhealthy. This is not the Mexico I know. Yes, the Mexicans are masters in rich, succulent, chilli-spiked meat braises and great seafood, and yes, as with so many diets worldwide, there has certainly been a steady shift to higher meat consumption. However, the indigenous Aztec diet was a celebration of vegetables and other plant-life, full of beans (uniquely rich in fibre and protein), corn (full of essential vitamins and minerals) and vegetables like chillies, tomatoes and squash, which together provided almost all the nutrition needed for a healthy, complex diet.

This ancient diet is strikingly similar to many vegetarian and flexitarian diets being embraced around the world today; mainly plant-based with masses of protein naturally occurring from the beans, nuts and seeds. Occasionally wild birds, insects and fish from Mexico's long coastline added to the diet but it was largely vegetable-focused. Like so many other traditional cuisines around the world, Mexico's is centuries old but feels thrillingly modern.

So when it was suggested to me that I write a book full of tempting, colourful and joyful vegetable recipes inspired by one of my favourite countries, I was filled with excitement. As I set to planning this book my mind whirred and whizzed with ideas and possibilities like a Catherine Wheel at full throttle. We were in the middle of a grey, gloomy wintery lockdown and all I wanted to do was to get in the kitchen and start cooking.

We know we need to eat less meat if we are to curb carbon emissions; we know that we need to eat a greater diversity of vegetables for optimum gut health; food can play a huge part in the climate change puzzle so embracing a diet rich in vegetables feels like a wonderfully positive step in the right direction. I am flexitarian by choice (trying to eat little meat, produced with care for the animal and for the environment), but in this book I have focused purely on plants with a little dairy – and it is brimming with exciting vegetarian and vegan recipes that feel new and a bit different. For those who are strictly following a plant-based diet I have tried to annotate how easily you can turn many of the vegetarian recipes into vegan ones. I have included a small icon ⓥ on the recipes that are vegan, as well as recipes that have vegan options or are easily adaptable with my tips.

You will find recipes inspired by Mexico's bounty of ingredients (pumpkins, courgettes, tomatoes, etc.) and by its unique cooking methods from charring fruit and vegetables for depth of flavour, grinding nuts and seeds into sauces for substance, to using huge handfuls of herbs in salsas, sauces and soups. Take the Wild Greens Spring Soup on page 114 – it is a simplified take on Oaxaca's traditional *sopa de guia*, a soup that pays homage to the courgette plant, teaming with its young, tender leaves, shoots, fruit and flowers and studded with a few kernels of white corn, plentiful herbs and a drizzle of deliciously seasoned chilli sauce. Some of the simple, but exotic tasting sauces and simple moles [moll-ays] in this book are enriched with ground nuts, sesame and pumpkin seeds, just as the Aztecs did, while others are just gently seasoned with some of the spices in the Mexican cook's repertoire: allspice, cinnamon, clove and cumin.

We will never be able to cook with all the wonderful produce Mexico has to offer outside Mexico, so I find alternatives when I can and otherwise try to respect Mexican food and culture as much as I can. There are tacos and enchiladas filled with seasonal vegetables that I find in my shops and local markets, just as Mexican cooks fill their tacos, stews and other dishes with the wild mushrooms, artichokes, greens and courgettes that are grown around them. You will learn how to add flavour to your food with a handful of my favourite Mexican chillies and herbs and how to prepare seasonal salads and pickles in just the way they are cooked and prepared in modern Mexican cantinas, brasseries, cafes and restaurants. There are plenty of delicious puddings made with fruit, vanilla and chocolate but you will also get an insight into the delicious breakfasts you can cook in an authentic but wholly vegetarian manner.

This book, if I have done my job, will suck you in with its colour, its vivacity and its tempting collection of recipes. Mexico has the most magical of cuisines that is subtle yet gutsy, nuanced and bold, packed full of flavour, that is often not spicy but always served with a spirit of conviviality. I do hope you will cook and love the recipes in this book as I have done.

THOMASINA MIERS

NOTES ON INGREDIENTS

HERBS

Oaxaca is one of the most biodiverse states in a country renowned for its diversity of plant life. It was in the wholesale market of Oaxaca that I began to understand the wonder of this. On a tour of Oaxaca's wholesale market with Alejandro Ruiz, a well-known chef in the state, he explained some of the wild herbs and greens used in Oaxacan cooking. It was here that I first tried *sopa de guía*, a clear broth laden with all the edible parts of the courgette plant, plus handfuls of exotic herbs like epazote, chépil, hierba de conejo and hoja santa. In my cooking I use fresh herbs like chervil, chives, tarragon, parsley and dill to try to capture some of the essence of the harder-to-find ones, but more recently Mexican oregano and hoja santa have become available through specialist suppliers (see page 249).

MEXICAN OREGANO

Native to Mexico, this distinctively aromatic herb is not related to European oregano but rather to the lemon verbena plant. It has citrussy, woody, grassy undertones and is sweeter than European oregano. It adds flavour to sauces, stews and bean dishes but is also taken medicinally as it is rich in vitamins and minerals and is used to fight common colds, Alzheimer's and osteoporosis, amongst other things. It is now widely available in dried form from specialist retailers.

HOJA SANTA

Hoja santa grows all over central and southern Mexico and its large leaves are the perfect size to line tortillas, wrap around chillies and lay out under a frying egg. It is a fragrant, bewitching herb and is used to give sweet-savoury notes to breakfast eggs, sauces and guisados (stews). Its unusual flavour is hard to pin down with hints of liquorice, mint and tarragon. It is particularly good with the Charred Poblano Linguine on page 124. It has only recently become available in the dried form from MexGrocer, a discovery that made me jump for joy.

QUELITES, GREENS & EDIBLE FLOWERS

In Mexico, more than 250 plant species with edible stems, leaves, vines and flowers, known as *quelites,* are collected, cultivated and consumed. This is a country where it is totally normal for cooks to forage for edible plants and leaves to add to their recipes, and cooking with a wide range of greens and flowers is part of Mexican culture. Thanks to their abundance, it is quite normal to eat street food stuffed with blanched or sautéed greens or filled with courgette flowers, which are sold in huge sack loads for very little money. Other edible flowers include nasturtium, hibiscus, rose, orange blossom and countless other species. Buying edible flowers can be expensive, so if you have a windowsill, space for a pot or a small patch of ground, consider growing chives, nasturtiums, thyme or courgettes for an affordable but intensely pleasing way to add flowers to your cooking.

HIBISCUS FLOWERS

Known as *flor de Jamaica* in Mexico, this dried flower is most often used to make a soft drink called agua fresca. Its tart, slightly sour flavour is similar to cranberry and can be used to give a fruity tang to savoury sauces and dressings, rather like the Middle Eastern berry, sumac. It is available from specialist retailers and most Middle Eastern grocers. It is wonderful on the Orange Ricotta Doughnuts on page 190.

MILK & DAIRY

When I left Ballymaloe Cookery School in Ireland, I stayed in West Cork and worked at the Gubbeen cheese farm. There is something magical about the process of making cheese and I try to buy artisanal cheese when I can. I have become fascinated by how crucial a role grazing cattle can play in regenerating damaged soil and sinking carbon into it. Grass-fed dairy has an important part to play in our farming systems.

There are also some great non-dairy options now available in the shops and much of the Mexican diet is naturally light in dairy. Ground nuts and seeds add protein to creamy moles, as do the beans and pulses. Dairy is very often just a sprinkle here and there for texture, colour and a touch of creaminess. I like to finely grate cheese over dishes for flavour, unless of course cheese is the focal point of the dish, in which case I can go a bit wild.

CREMA

Mexican crema is a delicious, slightly soured cream that melts smoothly into soups without separating. It is used throughout Mexican cooking to soften the heat of fiery salsas and the intensity of rich moles. Sour cream and crème fraîche are great alternatives (although sour cream tends to separate in hot food). A recipe to make your own crema is on page 242.

MEXICAN CHEESES

With their fresh curd cheeses, melting string cheeses, goat's and cream cheeses, the dairy stands in Mexican markets are an impressive sight. When you consider that the diet of the Native Mexicans consisted largely of vegetables and corn, it is not surprising that dairy became an important part of their cuisine.

QUESO OAXAQUEÑO OR QUESILLO

In Mexico, Oaxacan string cheese, *quesillo*, is famous for its melting qualities and so is used in quesadillas and empanadas. At Wahaca we use a blend of Cheddar, mozzarella and other cheese.

QUESO FRESCO

A young, slightly tart cheese that is crumbled over many street foods and tastes somewhere between feta and Lancashire cheese.

QUESO ANEJO

An aged cheese, this is like a good pecorino, or other good-quality aged sheep's cheese.

REQUESÓN

Found throughout Mexico, this is like the ricotta you can buy in most delicatessens and larger supermarkets. It is worth buying good-quality ricotta and using it soon after you have bought it. In Mexico, *requesón* is used fresh or sautéed to fill chillies or courgette flowers or whipped with eggs and sugar to make delicious cakes.

CHILLIES & OTHER INGREDIENTS

The following are some ingredients that would be useful to have in your cupboards when cooking from this book. You do not have to get all of them, but a selection of some of them would be both useful and fun!

FRESH CHILLIES

JALAPEÑO – FIERY

Green and curvy, jalapeños can be quite spicy, although the heat fades quickly. Available in good greengrocers, especially in the summer, they are great in salsas or stuffed, then baked or deep-fried. You can substitute most fresh green chillies in their place or, if you like hot food, bird's eye chillies.

SERRANO – GRASSY, GREEN & HOT

Fresh and green like jalapeños, but smaller and skinnier, serranos are mainly used chopped or roasted in vibrant salsas like the classic salsa verde, a blend of garlic, tomatillos and serranos. You can order them by mail order during the summer, otherwise use jalapeños or any other fresh green chillies.

POBLANO – MILD

Poblanos look like green peppers but with darker, glossier skin. Poblanos are mostly mild in heat but have a fantastically 'green' vegetable taste, unlike any other chilli. They are generally roasted, peeled and either stuffed, blended into sauces or cut into strips to make *rajas*.

HABANERO (AND SCOTCH BONNET) – FRUITY & FEROCIOUSLY FIERY

Habaneros are about an inch across and look like brightly coloured Chinese lanterns, in hues of orange, red and green. They have a deliciously fruity flavour and a fierce heat, so you need to use them carefully to harness their irresistible combination of heat and taste. They can only be called habaneros if they are grown in the Yucatán and can be bought in salsas or dried. They are closely related to the Scotch bonnet, which is available in larger supermarkets.

DRIED CHILLIES

CASCABEL – MILD

Small, fat and round, cascabels are mild in heat with an earthy, rich intoxicating flavour. Dry-roasting brings out their nuttiness, making them ideal for tomato-based salsas and sauces. Often used alongside other chillies, such as chipotle, they famously rattle when shaken.

ANCHO – MEDIUM

Sweet and mild, this chilli adds an incredible sweetness and depth of flavour to stews and sauces when soaked in water and puréed or lightly fried. If you can't find them, use Nora chilli or Aleppo pepper.

ÁRBOL – HOT

A skinny dried red chilli, the árbol scatters an addictive sprinkling of dry chilli heat to soups, stews, chilli oils and pasta sauces. It is beautifully versatile: easy to toast, crumble or blend. Sprinkle into roasts and braises or use to spike roast nuts. If you don't have árbol, use pepperoncino, the small Italian chilli, or other dried chilli (hot pepper) flakes.

GUAJILLO – DEEP RED & MILD

This brick-red, mild-heated, smooth-skinned chilli has a lively, tangy flavour reminiscent of berries and green tea. Pronounced gua-hee-yo, it has a rather tough skin that needs a little more soaking than other chillies, but it makes a wonderful paste that will add a slightly sweet flavour to your food as well as a deep red colour.

CHIPOTLE – SMOKY AND FIERY

Dried chipotle chillies are often rehydrated and cooked into a sweet, smoky tomato and garlic-based paste called an 'adobo'. This staple lasts for months in the fridge and adds depth of flavour and complexity to sauces, stews, mayonnaises and dressings. It is easy to make and the home-made version (page 234) is infinitely better than anything you can buy, but if buying in the shop just add some brown sugar and fresh lime juice or red wine vinegar to bump up the flavour.

PIQUIN CHILLIES

Tiny, berry-like chillies that have a citrussy flavour and a quick burst of heat. They are usually ground and sprinkled over cocktail rims, fruits and vegetables.

URFA CHILLI FLAKES

A deep-flavoured chilli from Turkey with notes of chocolate. Widely available in the UK, it can be used in place of chillies like ancho and cascabel (although it is much hotter than the latter).

ACHIOTE

Achiote is a brick-red paste made from the ground seeds of the annato berry. Its tangy, fruity flavour is delicious and reminiscent of sumac.

TOMATILLOS

The tomatillo is related to the cape gooseberry with a light parchment casing and looks like a green tomato. Its tangy, citrussy fresh flavour is highly prized in Mexico and it is a pivotal ingredient in green salsas and for adding sharp, acidic notes to salsas and sauces.

PILONCILLO OR PANELA

Traditionally Mexican puddings are sweetened with *piloncillo*, a richly flavoured unrefined sugar cane with a sweet, nutty flavour. If you can't find it, most health food shops sell *rapadura* or *panela* sugar, which are also unrefined and considered to be healthier than refined sugar because of trace amounts of vitamins and minerals.

TORTILLAS

Gluten-free, full of flavour and essential vitamins and minerals, the corn tortilla is used to hold a multitude of delicious ingredients, or rolled up and used to scoop up food. Corn is grown all over Mexico but there are more varieties (in colours of white, blue, black, red and yellow) in the south. In northern Mexico the corn tortilla makes way for the flour one, which is larger, stretchier, rich in flavour and paper thin.

VINEGAR

Home-made vinegars are fantastic for a healthy gut microbiome and are found throughout Mexico. They are used extensively in pickles and for dressing slaws, preserving food and adding a lovely bright balance to slow-cooked braises. Popular types come from fermenting pineapple (page 214), guava or apple. Experiment with great-quality apple cider vinegars; good ones have a soft sweetness to them. I have also recently tasted a great agave vinegar.

LOCAL FOOD MARKETS & GROWING

Mexican food, more than anything else, is a celebration of plant life and the seasons. Edible flowers, tender greens, a diversity of corn, chillies, tropical fruit and vegetables; if the flavours of Mexico are extraordinary it is, for the most part, due to the exceptional nature of the produce, and their passionate cooks. So head to a local market and see what is in season. And if you are desperate for the bunches of courgette flowers you get in the Mexican markets, or some of the chillies, juicy tomatoes, or citrussy tomatillos, try sticking some seeds in the earth. Growing food will set you on your own journey, perhaps inspired by the incredible food culture of Mexico.

EQUIPMENT

And lastly, if you want to make life easier for yourself when recreating the recipes, it might be worth investing in the following bits of kit:

Tortilla press – for making your own tortillas
Griddle pan – for chargrilling
Pestle and mortar – for salsas and guacamole
A good upright food blender – for blitzing nuts, seeds and chillies for salsas and sauces.

FIRST LIGHT

When I think of daybreak in Mexico City, where I lived for a year in my twenties, I think back to early mornings with a chill in the air and the need for a warm sweater and a soft pair of trousers. The sun fights to get over the tall buildings and far-off mountain ranges but the day is full of promise, of hustle and bustle, as traders get up to go to the markets, street hawkers start advertising their wares on loudspeakers and people wake up to meet the new day.

I start the day with a simple vinegar tonic or gut-friendly shrub (in Mexico home-made fruit vinegars are a serious thing). On my way to work, after showering and gathering myself together, I might stop off at my favourite juice stand and pick up a juice blitzed with verdant greens and exotic fruit, a smoothie rich in small, sweet local bananas, oats and nuts, or a bowl of granola and yoghurt, sliced papaya, or a breakfast muffin.

If I am in a foodie neighbourhood, I will seek out a rich, dairy-free hot chocolate (see page 25) that provides the type of pick-me-up more akin to a caffeine fix, but with a softer, more gentle, cacao-rich high. This makes the perfect dunking ingredient for one of the sweet rolls that are baked fresh every morning. I will drink a lot, but I won't eat that much. I never do first thing and besides, I want to save my appetite for mid-morning eating, with a never-ending choice of delectable snacks and street foods. After all, in Mexico, lunch is not until 3pm, so there is a lot of morning to build up and sate one's appetite before building it up once more.

CACAO, CINNAMON & MAPLE GRANOLA

A cacao-laced toasted granola with hints of cinnamon and coconut. Try using date syrup instead of maple for a deeper flavour. Double up the recipe at Christmas time as this makes an amazing present, wrapped up in bags with fun ribbons.

MAKES 1KG (2¼LBS) (vo)

1 tsp ground cinnamon

2 tbsp cacao powder

1 tsp sea salt, plus more for sprinkling

125ml (4fl oz) olive oil

70ml (2½fl oz) maple syrup

90g (3oz) light brown soft sugar

450g (1lb) mixed oats, barley and rye

75g (2½oz) pecans, roughly chopped

100g (3½oz) hazelnuts (filberts), roughly chopped

75g (2½oz) pumpkin seeds

75g (2½oz) sunflower seeds

75g (2½oz) coconut flakes

150g (5oz) raisins (or a mix of raisins and cranberries)

Preheat the oven to 140°C/120°C fan/275°F/gas 1. Line two baking trays with parchment paper.

In a large bowl whisk together the cinnamon, cacao powder, salt, oil, maple syrup and sugar. Add all the dry ingredients and stir well to coat everything in the sticky stuff.

Spread out evenly on the trays – you are looking for thin layers so that the ingredients cook evenly; if they are piled up, they won't cook as well. Bake in the oven for 1 hour, stirring every 15 minutes so that the oats cook evenly. It is easier to take the trays out when you do this, so you don't lose heat from the oven.

The granola is ready when everything is looking golden. Leave to cool completely on the trays, sprinkle with sea salt and then pack up in jars or, if you are giving it away, in small bags with ribbons and handwritten labels.

Stored in an airtight container, the granola will keep for 4–6 weeks.

A JUICE, A TONIC & A SMOOTHIE

When I lived in Mexico City, I drank juices on my way into work every morning. They are hard to resist when the street vendors make them in front of your eyes with blended papaya, fresh lime, pineapple, guava and the rest. My regular stand, on the corner of Calle Tabasco, was run by a woman called Carmen who sported amazing eyeliner that framed large, twinkly eyes.

In the UK however, I rarely did breakfast juices. Somehow, I felt that they were a needless injection of sugar that I'd rather I ingested as a treat in the form of chocolate or sticky buns, or at least paired with some kind of fibre to slow down the sugar spikes. However over the last few years I have discovered a couple of morning drinks I love, which you'll find on the following pages. All three are dairy-free.

My mother has been taking cider vinegar for years for her arthritis and my kids think it is the best thing in the world! She laces it with farmhouse apple juice and flaxseeds and feeds them teaspoonfuls in the morning. They crowd around her, mouths open, like baby birds. It is a brilliant way to start the day with all of its probiotic qualities.

Another joy is the green juice that I became hooked on in Mexico City. I have it when I have had a late night or have been working too hard and my body is thirsting for green goodness. It feels incredibly restorative and has a gentle sweetness that I wouldn't do without.

Lastly, there is the banana smoothie. This is essentially like having a mini breakfast with oats, almonds and banana, but in liquid form. Sweet from the bananas and dates with substance (and protein) from the oats and nuts; yet refreshing and light with the water and fresh lime, it will sustain you for several hours without leaving you feeling weighed down. I think I could drink this every morning for a pretty long time before getting bored.

MY MOTHER'S CIDER TONIC

A zingy, health-affirming way to start the day, with cider vinegar for a healthy gut and flaxseeds to aid the digestive system.

MAKES 1 GLASS (VO)

2 tsp cider vinegar

1 heaped tsp flaxseeds

150–200ml (5–7fl oz) apple juice

Put the ingredients in a glass, stir and drink. If you are organised enough to make it the night before, it is supposed to be even better for you, but frankly I never get there.

GREEN WAKE-UP JUICE

Green, fresh-tasting goodness in a glass.

MAKES 3 GLASSES (VO)

3 celery sticks, peeled and roughly chopped

¼ cucumber, roughly chopped

200ml (7fl oz) cloudy apple juice

juice of 2 limes

small handful of mint leaves

small handful of flat-leaf (Italian) parsley, roughly chopped

Put the celery, cucumber, apple and lime juices into the blender and whizz until completely blended, then add the herbs and whizz again. If you have a juicer, just put everything through that. Drink at once.

BANANA, DATE & OAT SMOOTHIE

Smooth, creamy, citrussy and fresh all at once. I don't always feel ready to eat first thing in the morning, but this goes down a treat and feels like a beautifully nourishing way to get out into the day.

MAKES 1 GLASS (VO)

50g (2oz) whole blanched almonds

30g (1oz) oats

20–30g (1oz) de-stoned dates

4 tsp lime juice from 1 juicy lime

110g (4oz) ripe banana, peeled

handful of ice

Soak the almonds, oats and dates in 150ml (5fl oz) water for 30 minutes or or overnight. Scoop out the softened solids, leaving the soaking water in the bowl, and blitz them in an upright blender, adding the lime juice and tablespoons of the oaty soaking water to loosen the blades. Blend until you have a smooth liquid.

Add the banana and ice and blitz for a minute more. Serve over more ice. This lasts well in the fridge for several days.

HOT CHOCOLATE

Centuries ago, steaming cups of hot chocolate made with ground cacao, spices, chillies, nuts and hot water (not milk) would be handed out to Aztec and Mixtec warriors before they went into battle to give them some va-va-voom and, in ayurvedic medicine, is said to lend focus and creativity to the drinker. Made well, Mexican hot chocolate produces a rich, espresso-like buzz. An overly sweet hot chocolate with little cacao, and too much milk, does the reverse.

What one needs in hot chocolate is plenty of cacao (yes! The good stuff!), preferably both in powdered form and solid, which contains the cocoa butter. The chocolate itself is brimming with beneficial antioxidants and essential minerals. So, banish thoughts of hot chocolate being 'naughty' and think like a Mexican. Make it properly, with plenty of the chocolate and rejoice in its power to pick you up in the morning, at night, or at any other time of day.

LIKE WATER FOR CHOCOLATE

Like the original Aztec hot chocolate, this uses water, not milk, ground almonds and cinnamon. It is extremely rich so is best drunk in small quantities. I have left out the chillies, but you could always add them in if you feel like it.

MAKES 3–4 SMALL CUPS

30g (1oz) whole blanched almonds, soaked overnight in water

1 tsp ground cinnamon

1 tbsp cocoa powder (preferably raw)

1 tbsp soft brown sugar, honey or agave syrup

30g (1oz) dark (bittersweet) chocolate (go for your favourite 70%)

Drain the almonds and empty them into a small food processor with the cinnamon and cacao powder. Grind for a few minutes to a fine paste. Scrape out with a spatula into a small saucepan with the sugar and chocolate.

Pour in 400ml (14fl oz) water and warm over a medium heat, whisking, until the chocolate is steaming.

Serve in small cups as it is fabulously rich. For breakfast bliss, dunk in the warm Coffee Cardamom Pecan Morning Buns on page 28.

MY NIGHT-OWL HOT CHOCOLATE

Made with milk but still with a high cacao content, this is more mellow than the one with water, but it still produces that feel-good buzz. To be planetary friendly, try a grass-fed cows' milk or oat milk here.

MAKES 1 CUP

1 heaped tsp cocoa powder (preferably raw)

220ml (7½fl oz) milk (oat, coconut or cows')

10g (¼oz) dark (bittersweet) chocolate (go for your favourite 70%)

soft brown sugar, maple syrup or honey, to taste

Put the cacao powder into a cup and pour over a tablespoon of milk. Stir into a paste and then slowly add the rest of the milk, stirring all the time.

Empty into a non-stick saucepan and put over a medium heat with the chocolate.

Whisk with a silicone whisk until the chocolate has melted and the milk is hot. Pour into your cup and taste. You may only need ½ teaspoon of sugar, syrup or honey.

Sip and wait for the warm glow and rush of energy to kick in.

BANANA BREAKFAST MUFFINS

These quick, simple muffins are totally delicious and last well in a bread bin or tin for several days. Eat as they are or, for something a little more indulgent, serve them with pumpkin seed butter and berries. And when blueberries are in season, swap them in for the raisins.

MAKES 12 MUFFINS (VO)

320g (11½oz) ripe bananas, peeled

80ml (2½floz) olive oil or other mild oil, plus more for greasing

90g (3oz) light brown soft sugar

1 tsp vanilla bean paste or extract

190g (7oz) wholemeal spelt flour

3 tsp baking powder

2 tsp ground cinnamon

½ tsp salt

30g (1oz) rolled (porridge) oats

50g (2oz) sunflower seeds, plus extra to top the muffins

50g (2oz) raisins or blueberries (when in season)

TO FINISH

Pumpkin Seed Butter and berries

Preheat the oven to 190°C/170°C fan/375°F/gas 5. Grease and line a 12-hole muffin tin.

Slice 12 banana discs and put to one side. Mash the remaining bananas in a mixing bowl, and then add the oil, sugar and vanilla. Mix well.

Use a sieve to add the flour, baking powder, cinnamon and salt. Combine gently with a metal spoon before adding the oats, seeds and raisins or blueberries to the mix.

Divide the mixture among the muffin holes, approximately 2 heaped tablespoons per muffin. Place a slice of banana on the top of each muffin and sprinkle over the extra sunflower seeds. Bake for 15–20 minutes or until the muffins have risen and are springy to touch. Serve with the pumpkin seed butter (see below) and berries.

FOR THE PUMPKIN SEED BUTTER

Preheat the oven to 190°C/170°C fan/375°F/gas 5. Spread 250g (9oz) pumpkin seeds out in a single layer on a baking (cookie) sheet and roast for 12 minutes. Leave to cool before adding to a food processor along with 2–3 tablespoons of maple syrup and 1 teaspoon of sea salt. Blend the seeds in 4–5-minute intervals, stopping the machine and allowing it to rest to prevent it overheating. Scrape down the sides of the machine at each interval and blend until smooth, about 20 minutes in total. Once smooth, taste and add more salt if needed.

Stored in an airtight container in the fridge, the pumpkin seed butter will last for up to 4–6 months in the fridge.

ROAST STRAWBERRY, MAPLE & BALSAMIC CHIA POTS

Not only does this make a wonderful breakfast when strawberries are in season, it makes a quick-and-easy pudding too. If you are feeding this to children don't be alarmed by initial rejections: my older two children took some time getting used to the consistency of chia.

SERVES 2–3 (vo)

4g (⅛oz) dried hibiscus flowers

50g (2oz) chia seeds

220ml (7½fl oz) cows' or coconut milk (the drinking kind, not the tins for cooking)

500g (1lb 2oz) strawberries

1 tsp vanilla extract

zest and juice of 1 lime

2 tbsp maple syrup

1 tsp balsamic vinegar

20g (¾oz) coconut flakes

150g (5oz) Greek or coconut yoghurt

Preheat the oven to 220°C/200°C fan/425°F/gas 7.

Empty the hibiscus flowers into a spice grinder and blitz to a fine powder.

Put the chia seeds in a mixing bowl with the milk and stir.

Wash and hull the strawberries. Empty half of them into a lined baking dish and toss with the hibiscus, vanilla, half the lime juice and zest and half the maple syrup. Sprinkle over the balsamic vinegar and roast for 20–30 minutes until tender and jammy. Toast the coconut flakes on a separate tray in the oven for about 5 minutes until golden.

Meanwhile, roughly chop the remaining strawberries and roughly mash them with the rest of the lime and maple syrup. Stir this through the chia seeds and taste to check the sweetness. Fold through the yoghurt and spoon into small glasses. Top with the balsamic-roasted strawberries and their juices, then sprinkle with the toasted coconut flakes.

COOK'S NOTE For extra creaminess you can use tinned coconut milk if you are making this for a pudding.

COFFEE, CARDAMOM & PECAN MORNING BUNS

Breakfast is taken seriously in Mexico and going out for it is a pastime that can take hours. I am a sucker for these buns which are an ode to the tradition of breakfast buns brought out with the hot chocolate, coffee and fresh juices first course. Yum.

MAKES 12 BUNS

FOR THE DOUGH

50g (2oz) butter

250ml (9fl oz) whole milk

500g (1lb 2oz) strong white flour, plus extra for dusting

50g (2oz) caster (superfine) sugar

1 tsp ground cardamom

1 tsp salt

1 x 7g (¼oz) fast-action yeast sachet

1 egg, beaten

olive oil, for greasing

FOR THE FILLING

100g (3½oz) butter, softened

60g (2oz) light brown soft sugar

2 tsp ground cinnamon

150g (5oz) pecans, chopped

1 egg, beaten

1 tsp salt

FOR THE COFFEE GLAZE

3 tbsp espresso or strong filtered coffee

2 tbsp caster (superfine) sugar

COOK'S NOTE These are also delicious with a citrus glaze. Mix 1 tablespoon of fresh lime juice, 1 tablespoon of fresh orange juice and their zests with 4 tablespoons of caster (superfine) sugar. Dissolve and brush over the warm buns or brush over melted Seville orange marmalade in homage to the Seville orange trees brought to Mexico by the Spanish.

To make the dough, melt the butter in a pan, then pour into the milk. Place all the dry ingredients in a large bowl (or the bowl of a processor with a dough hook). Mix thoroughly and make a well in the centre. Pour in the butter mixture and the egg.

Use your hands (or the dough attachment on a mixer) to bring together to a smooth dough. Add a dash of milk if needed. Tip out onto a very lightly floured surface and knead for 5–10 minutes (or 3–4 minutes if using a mixer) until stretchy and smooth. Lightly oil the mixing bowl and add the dough, cover and leave until doubled in size (between 1–2 hours).

To make the filling, mix the butter, sugar and cinnamon together until well combined.

Once the dough has doubled in size, return to the floured surface and roll out to a rectangle approx. 20 x 30cm (8 x 12 inches). Spread the filling evenly onto the dough and sprinkle over the pecans. Roll the dough lengthways as tightly as you can, wrap in parchment paper and refrigerate for 30 minutes.

Line a 20 x 30cm (8 x 12 inch) baking tray with parchment paper. Cut the roll into 12 slices and place on the prepared tray, tucking the end of the spiral underneath. Cover and leave to prove for a further 45 minutes.

Preheat the oven to 200°C/180°C fan/400°F/gas 6.

Combine the egg and salt and brush over the buns then bake in the preheated oven for 15 minutes. Turn the tin and bake for a further 10 minutes.

To make the glaze, add the coffee and the sugar to a small pan over a medium heat with 1 tablespoon of water. Cook for 5 minutes or until syrupy.

Remove the buns from the oven and immediately pour over the glaze. These are best eaten fresh, but will keep in an airtight container for 1–2 days.

OVERNIGHT OATS FOR ALL SEASONS

I like to start the day slowly when it comes to food. I only really build up a proper appetite by mid-morning or towards lunch, unless I have been out late-night dancing (those were the days). But I do often want something small and light before dashing out of the house or for mid-morning at work.

Overnight oats are the perfect answer. Made the night before, they can be wolfed down in small quantities, they don't feel too heavy and can be ladled into old jam jars and taken into work for when you need it. Soaking them overnight unlocks the nutrients by making them easier to digest. My children lap them up and anything to get them away from sugary breakfast cereals is a bonus.

As I write this, I can close my eyes and transport myself back to Mexico City. In the morning I would walk to the cocktail bar I ran and on my way stop at a breakfast fruit stand that made thick fruit purées, juices, smoothies, oats and granolas, peppered with protein-rich chia and amaranth seeds scattered over the tropical fruit. These are my versions, using apples, peaches and cherries in place of the papayas, pineapples and guavas that I ate in vast quantities when I was over there. Take me back. Please take me back.

MY BASE

This recipe can use any oats, including barley, rye and even quinoa flakes, and can use any type of milk or water for a lighter finish. The oats can be topped with stone fruit, rhubarb compote or diced fresh fruit. Have fun making and eating them!

THIS RECIPE MAKES ENOUGH FOR 4–5 HELPINGS

125g (4½oz) oats (rolled porridge oats, jumbo oats or a mix with barley/rye flakes)

70g (2½oz) nuts or seeds (see suggestions opposite)

2 tsp ground cinnamon or 1 tsp ground cardamom

50g (2oz) honey, maple syrup or agave syrup

zest and juice of ½ lemon

200ml (7fl oz) any type of milk or water, plus extra to loosen

200g (7oz) plain, Greek, kefir or coconut yoghurt

Put all the ingredients straight into the container you are using to store them overnight.

Put in the fridge overnight or for a minimum of 4–5 hours. Check the consistency in the morning and add water or milk to loosen the mixture to the consistency you like, adjusting the sweetness to your taste.

Once soaked overnight, this base will keep for 4–5 days in the fridge.

ROAST PLUMS & TARRAGON

In the autumn I love to top the oats with roast plums. They are a sensation, turning a deep, dark pink in the oven, which stains the oats with such vivid colour that it feels an incredibly life-affirming way to start the day.

Preheat the oven to 190°C/170°C fan/375°F/gas 5. Toss 400g (14oz) stoned plums in a baking dish with 2 tbsp water and 2 tsp maple syrup or brown sugar and ½ tsp vanilla extract. Roast for 15–20 minutes or until softened and looking jammy. Remove from the oven and scrape the fruit and its jammy roasting juices into your container. Add 1 tbsp finely chopped tarragon and proceed with the main recipe opposite, using your choice of nuts and seeds.

APPLE, CARDAMOM & HAZELNUTS

Closest to a Bircher muesli of all these overnight oats, this is the classic one I turn to with my love of a good apple. It makes a wonderful, fresh but sustaining start to the day. Find interesting varieties of apples at farmers' markets and farm shops, or online, over the autumn and winter – they taste a million times better than the few standard varieties sold in supermarkets.

Grate 2 large apples (or pears) into the container you are using to store the oats. Omit the milk and use 200ml (7fl oz) apple juice instead, ½ tsp ground cardamom and a mix of toasted hazelnuts and sunflower seeds. Adjust the sweetness to your taste.

PEACH, RASPBERRY, COCONUT & PECAN

These are only worth making for 3 months over the summer when peaches or nectarines are in their prime. They are nonetheless a glorious way to eat these sticky, juicy wonder fruits. The raspberries are a lovely Melba-esque way to finish the oats.

Using a coarse grater, grate 2 large ripe peaches or nectarines straight into a large container, stopping when you get to the core. Stir in a mix of toasted pecans and pumpkin seeds and 35g (1oz) desiccated (dried shredded) coconut, along with ½ tsp ground cinnamon (or more to taste). The next morning, adjust the sweetness, loosen with more milk or water and top with 50g (2oz) raspberries.

CHERRY, TOASTED ALMOND & STAR ANISE

A celebration of cherries and their short season, I would eat these the whole year round if I could, with their deep cherry-stained hues seeping into the oats. Hell, yes.

De-stone 200g (7oz) cherries over a big container, making sure you catch all the juices and ripping them into smaller pieces as you let them fall into the bowl. Stir in the rest of the ingredients, plus 50g (2oz) toasted flaked almonds, 25g (1oz) flaxseeds and ¼ tsp ground star anise. The next day, top with extra cherries and toasted almonds before eating.

COOK'S NOTE Also great with roast rhubarb, ginger, lemon zest (although you will need a touch more sugar), apricot and cinnamon.

BREAKFAST FLAPJACKS

Just the ticket for when you are running out the door but want to take something relatively healthy with you to munch when hunger bites. These are a doddle to prepare and even my children, allergic to anything they think of as 'healthy', love them. Any dried fruit and nut combo works here. Try dried pineapple with the coconut for a fun pairing, or tone down a seed for more almonds here to complement the cherries.

MAKES 16 FLAPJACKS (vo)

180g (6½oz) coconut oil

180g (6½oz) soft brown sugar

4 tbsp golden (light corn) syrup

80g (3oz) coconut flakes

250g (9oz) jumbo oats

2 tsp ground cinnamon

1 tbsp chia seeds

80g (3oz) mix of sunflower, pumpkin and sesame seeds

50g (2oz) flaked (slivered) almonds

80g (3oz) sour cherries, roughly chopped

sea salt

Preheat the oven to 200°C/fan 180°C/400°F/gas 6. Line a 25 x 30cm (10 x 12 inch) baking tin with parchment paper.

Melt the coconut oil in a small pan, take off the heat and mix in the sugar and golden syrup.

Meanwhile, put the coconut flakes and a third of the oats into a food processor and blitz to a fairly fine crumb. In a large bowl, add all the other flapjack ingredients and mix well before adding the coconut and sugar mixture. Season with several pinches of sea salt.

Transfer the mixture to the prepared tin, pat the mixture down and smooth over for a level top.

Bake for 15–20 minutes until golden. Wait for the flapjacks to cool a little before slicing into squares. They will keep in an airtight container for up to 2 weeks but never last that long!

SQUIDGY PEANUT BUTTER & CHOCOLATE COOKIES

The street hawkers in Mexico City sell small peanut marzipans which for a time held me entirely in their snare. Peanuts come from the Americas and when ground, they add a delicious flavour to savoury moles and puddings. Here, their taste comes alive in a soft cookie seasoned with sea salt and studded with chunks of dark chocolate. They are totally irresistible. If I wanted to start the day with something wicked, I would want to start with these.

MAKES 12–14 COOKIES

220g (8oz) white spelt flour

1 tsp baking powder

½ tsp bicarbonate of soda (baking soda)

½ tsp sea salt

140g (5oz) unsalted butter, softened

100g (3½oz) light brown soft sugar

100g (3½oz) caster (superfine) sugar

2 eggs

120g (4½oz) peanut butter

1½ tsp vanilla extract

150g (5oz) dark (bittersweet) chocolate chunks

Mix the flour, baking powder, bicarbonate of soda and salt together in a medium bowl. Set aside.

Using a hand mixer or a stand mixer fitted with a paddle attachment, cream the butter and both sugars together on medium speed until smooth, about 1–2 minutes. Don't overbeat or your cookies will rise and then sink again. Add the eggs to the mix, one at a time, beating to combine. Scrape down the sides and bottom of the bowl and then beat in the peanut butter and vanilla for a minute until fully mixed in.

Remove the paddle and fold in the dry ingredients and chocolate. Taste and add a little more sea salt to season if needed (it seasons them and offsets the sweetness). The dough will be thick and soft, so move the bowl to the fridge for 30–40 minutes to set.

Once the dough is less soft, scoop out roughly 1½ tablespoons of dough to make roughly 60g (2¼oz) pieces. If you measure the first couple, you will soon get the hang of the size. Roll each of these pieces into a ball, lay on a parchment-lined baking sheet and freeze for at least a few hours or overnight.

When you are ready to eat, preheat the oven to 180°C/160°C fan/350°F/gas 4. Line a second baking sheet with parchment paper and arrange the balls, allowing plenty of space to spread, so about 6–8 per sheet. Cook for 15 minutes from frozen or 13 minutes if you have allowed them to defrost for 5–10 minutes before. These are irresistible, so make as many as you want to eat and leave the rest in the freezer for the next time you have a cookie attack!

COOK'S NOTE It helps to use a lower-quality peanut butter here, so if you only have a good one, blitz 100g (3½oz) peanut butter with 1 heaped tablespoon of melted butter or vegetable oil to soften it.

BREAKFAST, BRUNCH, ANYTIME

If my days start lightly with a juice or a drinking vinegar; a shrub or a smoothie; tea followed by coffee, by mid-morning my stomach starts to rumble in earnest.

The rhythm of breakfast in Mexico will start with a fresh juice, hot chocolate or coffee, as you might expect, but it will swiftly move on to proper sustenance. Some warm pastries, fresh from the oven, and platters of tropical fruit. Then the savoury courses follow. Eggs in so many guises: scrambled, fried, turned over with salsas, sauces and moles, and bumped up with vegetables to keep you going until lunch, which is often taken at three in the afternoon.

This later style of breakfasting suits me perfectly. At weekends it means we can have friends over and turn out piles of fluffy lime-flecked ricotta pancakes, or a last-minute banana and chocolate cornbread. After a late night, we want something with more substance – a plate of chipotle baked eggs to scoop up with tortillas, or a light but nourishing breakfast burrito. Even in the week, I will come down after a few hours of writing and prepare something on the fly: some tofu quickly turned in a pan with chipotles and tomatoes or a loose heap of just-cut tomatoes tossed in fresh lime and chilli and heaped onto garlic-rubbed toast. These plates are designed to satisfy the first real hunger pangs of the day and are all about taste and deep, pleasing sustenance.

SMOKY CHIPOTLE TOFU
WITH CHERRY TOMATOES & AVOCADO

An intensely smoky, warm chilli-tossed tofu against a soothing, cool, smashed avocado – this is incredible on toast and even better inside a breakfast taco.

FEEDS 2–3 (vo)

SMOKY CHIPOTLE TOFU

2 tbsp olive oil

225g (8oz) block smoked firm tofu, cut into small cubes

3 tbsp Chipotles en Adobo (page 234)

3 spring onions (scallions) (50g/2oz), finely sliced

150g (5oz) cherry tomatoes, halved

Smashed Avocado (see below)

sea salt

SMASHED AVOCADO

1 large avocado

zest and juice of 1 lime or ½ lemon

salt and pepper

AND POSSIBLY ...

garlic cloves

chilli oil or Korean chilli flakes

chopped coriander (cilantro), chervil, tarragon, basil or dill

drizzle of tahini

Heat a frying pan (skillet) over a medium–high heat and when hot, add the oil followed by the tofu. Fry for a few minutes to crisp, then add the chipotle. Stir-fry for another few minutes, seasoning with at least ½ teaspoon of sea salt, before adding the spring onions and cherry tomatoes. Turn the heat down to medium and cook for 7–8 minutes until the tomatoes are beginning to break down a little. Taste and adjust the seasoning, then serve on a bed of smashed avocado, in a taco or on toast.

SMASHED AVOCADO

The simplest of starts to the day. Cut the avocado in half and discard the stone. Mash the garlic, if using, with ½ teaspoon of salt with a knife or pestle and mortar. Mash with the avocado flesh and add the citrus and chilli, herbs or tahini, if using. Taste, adjust the seasoning and serve.

You could experiment by mixing the avocado with tahini, black pepper and lemon juice; use 50:50 avocado and pea (page 62) or avocado and broad (fava) bean; top with tofu, tomatoes or tarragon. The beauty of avocado is that as well as being delicious with a simple sprinkling of salt, chilli and citrus, it is also a great foil for so many other ingredients.

BREAKFAST CHILAQUILES
WITH FRESH TOMATILLO SALSA

Chilaquiles, one of Mexico's most treasured recipes, was invented to use up stale tortillas and leftover salsa. In Mexico, there is always salsa about and chilaquiles is all about the salsa. Here I make a zingy, citrussy tomatillo one, which is particularly delicious when tomatillos are in season from June until late September, but you can also use tinned tomatillos. The natural accompaniment is a fried egg, although you can pair with refried beans and crema (page 242) or ricotta.

SERVES 4 (VO)

200g (7oz) leftover tortillas or good-quality plain tortilla chips

300g (10oz) fresh tomatillos or 350g (12½oz) tinned

1 white onion, cut into 8 wedges

3 garlic cloves, unpeeled

1 jalapeño chilli, de-stemmed

25g (1oz) coriander (cilantro), leaves and stalks

1 tbsp caster (superfine) sugar

2 tbsp olive oil

500ml (17fl oz) vegetable stock or water

juice of ½ lime

salt

SERVING SUGGESTIONS

4 fried eggs

sliced avocado

sour cream

few handfuls of coriander (cilantro) leaves

crumbled feta or Lancashire cheese

finely chopped red onion, Pink Pickled Onions (page 238) or Burnt Spring Onion Relish (page 238)

COOK'S NOTE When you buy corn tortillas, bag any leftovers and freeze for this dish. Otherwise, make with good-quality packet tortilla chips, but go lighter with the seasoning.

If using up tortillas, cut them into triangles, pour a few tablespoons of oil into a pan over a medium–high heat and shallow-fry until crisp.

If you have fresh tomatillos, remove their husks and wipe them with a damp cloth. Put a large frying pan (skillet) over a medium–high heat and dry-toast the onion, garlic, jalapeño and tomatillos, if they are the fresh ones (page 244). Shake and turn frequently until charred all over and tender in the middle, about 6–7 minutes for the garlic and chilli and a little longer for the onion and tomatillos. When cool enough to touch, peel the garlic and transfer to a blender along with the other charred ingredients and the coriander, sugar and 1½ teaspoons of salt. If you are using tinned tomatillos, add them at this point. Blitz the lot to a purée.

Warm the oil in a medium pan over a medium heat and pour in the sauce. Fry, stirring, for 2–3 minutes until it darkens slightly. Pour in the vegetable stock or water and bring to a simmering point. Squeeze in the lime juice, add the tortilla chips and toss gently in the sauce for just long enough for some of them to soften. Taste and adjust the seasoning if needs be, then remove from the heat and transfer to shallow bowls. Top with fried eggs and any of the other toppings or sides that you can gather together.

SUMMER TOMATOES ON TOAST

My eldest discovered tomatoes on toast for breakfast when she was eight and has never looked back. Sometimes I feel a little guilty as she trots off to school, oblivious to the scent of the garlic, but then I mentally shrug: at least she is eating the breakfast of kings! I love this with ajillo oil, a caramelised garlic and chilli oil, drizzled over. With or without the creamy ricotta base, this is a celebration of the tomato, the greatest of Mexican fruits, so seek out the ripest, best ones you can find and store them outside the fridge.

SERVES 2 (vo)

200g (7oz) mixed tomatoes

2–4 slices bread (the better the bread, the better your brekkie)

1 small garlic clove, peeled

2 tsp good-quality olive oil

small handful of tarragon or basil, chopped

salt and pepper

OPTIONAL EXTRAS

100g (3½oz) ricotta (page 106 for a herby one)

Ajillo Oil (page 236)

trickle of your favourite vinegar (page 17)

Cut the tomatoes into jaunty angles: a mixture of wedges, halves, quarters and slices will all do, depending on their size and your mood. Toast the bread over a griddle or in the toaster. Rub with the garlic and drizzle with the olive oil.

Spread with the ricotta, if using, and season it well with salt, pepper and a drizzle more oil. Top with the tomatoes, scatter over some herbs and drizzle with more olive oil or the ajillo oil and perhaps a little vinegar. Eat at once.

CHEESY BRUNCH BURRITOS
WITH AVO SALSA

These burritos are just the thing after a late night. If you are organised, you can have all but the avocado salsa done the night before, leaving you very little to do in the morning. Up the chillies if you need something fierce to blow through the cobwebs – they are rich in vitamin C and antioxidants, so they're perfect for a pep up.

SERVES 4

4–6 eggs, beaten

1 tsp smoked paprika, sweet or hot

2 spring onions (scallions), chopped

20g (¾oz) butter

60g (2oz) Cheddar cheese, grated

4 flour tortillas (page 245)

200g (7oz) warm Whole or Twice-cooked Beans (page 75), black or pinto

40g (1½oz) spinach

your choice of hot sauce or salsa (pages 226–31), to serve

FOR THE AVOCADO SALSA

1 large or 2 small avocados, de-stoned, peeled and cubed

¼ small red onion, finely chopped

2 handfuls of coriander (cilantro), roughly chopped

1 red chilli, finely chopped

juice of 1 lime

½ tsp ground cumin

salt and pepper

Put the avocados, onion, half the coriander, chilli, lime juice and ground cumin in a bowl, season generously and mix well.

Whisk together the eggs, paprika and spring onions and season with salt and pepper. Melt the butter in a saucepan over a low–medium heat and pour in the egg mix. Cook, stirring, for a minute, then stir in the cheese and continue to cook and stir until they are almost done. The eggs will carry on cooking after you have removed them from the heat and again in the tortilla.

Spoon 2 tablespoons of the avocado salsa into the middle of each tortilla and flatten slightly. Follow with a quarter of the beans, eggs and spinach, scrunching up the spinach in your hands to soften it. Fold the sides over the filling and roll, tucking in the edges as you go.

Place a griddle pan over a medium heat and when hot, add the burritos, seam-side down. Cook until golden and crisp, about 1–2 minutes each side. Serve halved with the remaining avocado salsa and your favourite hot sauce or salsa on the side.

SPINACH & THREE-CHEESE MOLLETE

Mollettes, the incredibly simple open sandwiches, are devoured enthusiastically by toddlers, teenagers and grown-ups alike; it is a brilliant recipe to have up your sleeve for when you need some good food fast. Sautéeing tinned beans in olive oil and garlic is child's play and means you can add aromatics to make them thrum with flavour (page 47). A good sourdough or ciabatta bun and the fresh tomato salsa are essential. Happy feasting.

SERVES 4

30g (1oz) butter, softened

large bag of spinach or Swiss chard

4 sourdough or ciabatta buns

100g (3½oz) mild goat's curd or cheese or ricotta

½ quantity of Twice-cooked Beans (page 75), warmed through

300g (10oz) mix of coarsely grated Cheddar, Poacher or other mature hard cheese

1 quantity of Fresh Tomato Pico (page 226)

salt and pepper

Preheat the grill.

Melt a knob of the butter in a hot pan and wilt the spinach or chard leaves until collapsed – this will take a few minutes. Season with salt and pepper. Cut the buns in half and toast the open sides in a hot, dry pan or under the grill. Butter both halves and then spread with goat's curd and then the twice-cooked beans. Top with the wilted leaves, sprinkle over the grated cheese and place under the grill until the cheese is bubbling and turning golden.

Top with a spoonful of pico and eat at once!

ALTERNATIVE

GARLICKY MUSHROOMS ON TOAST

The Garlic Mushrooms on page 147 make a deeply satisfying start to the day. I particularly love them on toast with the mild, chilli-spiked juices soaking into a delicious crumb, but it is also great on tacos. If you are going for broke, top with grated cheese and stick under the grill before serving.

SIMPLE BAKED BEANS

A delightfully easy baked bean recipe using a few tins of beans from the larder. You can make this the night before and simply warm it up the next day or make it first thing. Or try making this with dried varieties of beans you may have bought on your travels (or am I the only person who buys kilos of beans on holiday?!). Just as you put your phone on to charge at night, you can charge your dried beans in cold water to soak. They are easy to cook (page 247) and their texture is the silkiest of silks.

SERVES 6 (vo)

3 tbsp olive oil

1 large onion, finely chopped

2 celery sticks, finely chopped

2 fat garlic cloves, finely chopped

1–2 bay leaves

1 tsp dried oregano

1 tsp ground cinnamon

1 x 400g (14oz) tin chopped tomatoes

1 tsp Chipotles en Adobo (page 234) or 2 tsp smoked paprika

2 tbsp dark brown sugar

30g (1oz) dark (bittersweet) chocolate

1 tbsp soy sauce

2 tbsp red wine vinegar

2 x 400g (14oz) tins beans, such as borlotti, cannellini, white, pinto, Hodmedod's beans

salt and pepper

Preheat the oven to 180°C/160°C fan/350°F/gas 4. Warm the olive oil in an ovenproof pan over a medium heat and fry the onion and celery for 8–10 minutes until soft and sweet, seasoning generously with salt and pepper.

Add the garlic and fry for 2–3 minutes, then add the bay, oregano and cinnamon. Allow them to heat through, then add the rest of the ingredients and 300ml (10½fl oz) water. You will need to season again – try ½ teaspoon of salt and go from there – you can adjust the seasoning throughout cooking and at the end.

Bring to a simmer, then bake in the oven for 35–40 minutes until delicious and bubbling. Taste and adjust the flavour with salt, sugar, spice or vinegar. At this stage you can leave overnight and the dulcet flavours will mellow and improve, or eat at once with tortillas or on toast.

CHIPOTLE BAKED EGGS

The Mexican equivalent of a Middle Eastern shakshuka, this tomato-based smoky dish with baked eggs is a blissfully simple way to start the day, with all the pleasing, sweet, smoky flavours of a tomato-chipotle sauce. Mop up with tortillas or other flatbreads.

SERVES 4

3 tbsp olive oil

1 onion, finely sliced

2 garlic cloves, finely sliced

1 small red (bell) pepper, de-seeded and finely sliced

1 red chilli, finely chopped

1 tsp ground cumin

1 tsp ground cinnamon

1 tsp allspice

few large pinches of Mexican oregano or hoja santa (optional)

1 tbsp Chipotles en Adobo (page 234), or more to taste

2 x 400g (14oz) tins chopped tomatoes or 700g (1½lb) fresh tomatoes, chopped

2–3 tsp brown sugar

1 tbsp red wine vinegar

8 eggs

salt

TO SERVE

8 corn or flour tortillas (pages 245–6)

sliced avocado

handful of coriander (cilantro) leaves or chervil

Preheat the oven to 190°C/170°C fan/375°F/gas 5.

Warm the olive oil in a large ovenproof frying pan (skillet) over a medium heat – you can transfer to an ovenproof dish later. Add the onion, garlic, pepper and chilli. Season with a few pinches of salt and fry gently for 20 minutes until the pepper is soft and sweet.

Add the spices and herbs, if using, cook for another 30 seconds, then add the chipotle, tomatoes, sugar and vinegar with another big pinch of salt. The amount of sugar needed to season this will depend on whether you are using tinned or fresh tomatoes and their ripeness. Pour in 250ml (8fl oz) water, then simmer for 15 minutes until the sauce has reduced a little but you still have a lovely loose sauce for enveloping the eggs. Taste to check the seasoning.

Make small indents in the sauce and crack in the eggs. Bake in the oven for 12–15 minutes until the whites are just set.

While the eggs are cooking, warm the tortillas and serve with the avocado and torn coriander leaves.

SWEET POTATO RÖSTI

This giant rösti is a little like a Spanish tortilla, only we've ditched the Spanish vibe in favour of a Mexican party. Make the chimichurri while the sweet potatoes are sitting, and then relax with a cup of coffee and the papers. Before long, you will be having a feast. I like this with any kind of egg, whether fried, poached, or softly boiled.

SERVES 4 (vo)

2 large sweet potatoes (about 600g/1¼lb)

1 tsp sea salt

3 spring onions (scallions) (about 65g/2¼oz), finely sliced

30g (1oz) plain (all-purpose), white spelt or chickpea (gram) flour

1 tsp smoked paprika

1 egg, beaten

1 tbsp rapeseed (canola) oil

Quick Coriander Chimichurri Salsa (page 235)

soft-boiled eggs, to serve (optional)

FOR THE ROASTED TOMATOES

250g (9oz) cherry tomatoes on the vine

1 tsp sea salt

2 tbsp olive oil

You will need a well-seasoned heavy-bottomed or non-stick frying pan (skillet) with an ovenproof handle.

Peel the sweet potatoes and coarsely grate. Toss with the salt and leave in a colander for 1 hour. In the meantime, make the chimichurri salsa.

After an hour, preheat the oven to 190°C/170°C fan/375°F/gas 5. Put all the ingredients for the roasted tomatoes in a small baking dish and roast in the oven for 15–20 minutes.

Now, take a handful of the sweet potato mixture and squeeze the liquid out with your hands. Repeat this until the mixture you are left with is relatively dry. Add the spring onion to the sweet potato with the flour and paprika. Mix together until combined and then beat in the egg with a fork.

Heat the frying pan on a medium heat and add the oil. Add the rösti mixture and flatten into the pan. Cook on a low–medium heat for 8–10 minutes. Move the pan from the hob to the same oven as the tomatoes, putting the rösti on the top shelf. Bake for 15–20 minutes. Remove from the oven when the tomatoes are roasted and the rösti is golden brown.

Carefully turn the rösti out onto a plate before slicing and serving topped with roasted tomatoes, the eggs, if using, and a generous spoonful of chimichurri.

COOK'S NOTE For a vegan alternative, replace the egg with 1 tablespoon of flaxseeds mixed with 3 tablespoons of water and serve the rösti with Black Beans (page 75) and the Cashew Nut 'Crema' on page 242.

CHICKPEA RANCHEROS

This smoky, spicy, plant-based scramble is a brilliant substitute for scrambled eggs in a breakfast burrito or taco and, dare I say, tastes so good with the nutty chickpea flour that some of you who are not wild on eggs may even prefer it. I love serving this with the utterly delicious and mild Sweet Cascabel & Tomatillo Salsa on page 229, but it is also fantastic with Roast Chipotle Salsa (page 228), Salsa Macha (page 237) or Ajillo Oil (page 236). If you like Sicilian farinata, you will love this.

SERVES 4 (vo)

1 tbsp cider vinegar

½ tsp baking powder

150g (5oz) chickpea (gram) flour, mixed with 200ml (7fl oz) water at least 1 hour before cooking or the night before

2 tbsp olive oil

1 onion, chopped

2 garlic cloves, chopped

½ tsp ground cumin

½ tsp dried oregano

1 tsp Chipotles en Adobo (page 234)

1 x 400g (14oz) tin chickpeas, drained and rinsed

large handful of cherry tomatoes, quartered

salt and pepper

TO SERVE

handful of coriander (cilantro) leaves

warm tortillas (page 245)

your choice of salsa (pages 226–31)

Stir the vinegar and baking powder into the chickpea flour and water mix and put to one side.

Warm the olive oil in a frying pan (skillet) over a medium heat and add the onion and garlic. Season with a little salt and pepper and fry for 6–8 minutes until beginning to soften, then add the cumin, oregano, chipotle, chickpeas and half the tomatoes. Cook for a further 3 minutes or so to give the flavours time to mingle, then taste and adjust the seasoning.

Pour the chickpea mix into the pan and wait 20 seconds for it to begin to set before scraping the bottom of the pan with a wooden spoon. Add the remaining tomatoes and keep turning the pan and scraping until the mixture is scrambled to your liking, about 3 minutes.

Sprinkle with the coriander and serve with warm tortillas, salsa and all the bits and pieces.

SAVOURY QUINOA PORRIDGE

Much as I love normal porridge, which I make with various different oat, spelt, quinoa and barley flakes, there is something just as comforting about a savoury porridge. It always makes me think of Carolyn, who has worked with me at Wahaca for over a decade and whose Chinese roots always inform us about delicious Chinese delicacies, like the congee we once had together. Hodmedod's produce a British-grown quinoa, or try this with organic oats – both are great.

SERVES 4   (VO)

2 tbsp olive or rapeseed (canola) oil

1 onion, chopped

2 garlic cloves, chopped

1 tsp ground cumin

1 tsp ground cinnamon

1 tsp sweet paprika

1 tsp dried oregano

160g (5½oz) quinoa, rinsed thoroughly

salt

FOR THE TOFU

280g (10oz) firm tofu, drained

1 tbsp cornflour (cornstarch)

1 tsp sweet paprika

¼ tsp ground cinnamon

1 tbsp olive oil

TO SERVE

sliced avocado

2 big handfuls of coriander (cilantro) leaves

4 tbsp sour cream (optional)

4 tbsp salsa of your choice (pages 226–31)

4 fried eggs (optional)

Preheat the oven to 200°C/180°C fan/400°F/gas 6.

Warm the oil in a large pan and add the onion, garlic and a big pinch of salt. Cook for 6–7 minutes until soft, then add the spices and oregano. Cook for a moment to warm through, then add the rinsed quinoa, 1½ teaspoons of salt and 1 litre (1 quart) of water.

Bring to the boil, then turn the heat down and simmer for 30 minutes until the quinoa is completely soft. Taste and adjust the seasoning until you are happy.

While the quinoa is cooking, prepare the tofu. Pat dry with a paper towel and cut into 2cm (¾ inch) cubes. Place in a bowl and sprinkle over the cornflour, paprika, cinnamon, olive oil and some seasoning. Toss gently to coat, then lay out on a parchment-lined baking tray and place in the oven for 25–30 minutes until crisp.

Spoon the quinoa into bowls, then top with the tofu, avocado, coriander, sour cream, salsa and fried eggs, as you like.

FLUFFY RICOTTA PANCAKES

WITH CHIA, RASPBERRY & HIBISCUS JAM

These quick and simple fluffy pancakes remind me of the Scotch pancakes I loved as a child. You can top them with any of the usual pancake toppings, but they are particularly good with this raspberry & hibiscus jam, made with chia seeds, which dramatically cuts down the need for sugar to set it. Sharp berries and creamy, lime-flecked ricotta pancakes – yum. And the children don't even know that they are relatively healthy – that's a definite win!

SERVES 4, MAKES ABOUT 14 PANCAKES

250g (9oz) ricotta

75ml (2½fl oz) whole milk

2½ tbsp caster (superfine) sugar

zest of 1 lime

2 eggs, separated

75g (2½oz) plain (all-purpose) flour

1 tsp baking powder

butter, to cook

Greek yoghurt, to serve

FOR THE RASPBERRY JAM

10g (¼oz) dried hibiscus flowers (optional but good)

250g (9oz) fresh or frozen raspberries

4 tbsp maple syrup, honey or sugar

35g (1oz) chia seeds

½ tsp vanilla extract

COOK'S NOTE Experiment with different chia jams, depending on what is in season: blackberry and lime; cherry and vanilla; rhubarb and ginger; pear, lemon zest and cardamom. Chia jam is a deliciously quick way to enjoy seasonal fruits.

To make the jam, empty the hibiscus flowers (if using) into a spice grinder and blitz to a fine powder.

Put the berries and sweetener into a small pan and sift in the hibiscus, discarding the larger pieces that remain behind in the sieve. Pour in 100ml (3½fl oz) water and simmer for 5 minutes, using a potato masher to break down the raspberries. Once broken down and beginning to bubble again, take off the heat and stir in the chia and vanilla. Leave to rest and cool while you prepare the pancakes. The jam will set in a few hours in the fridge and keep in an airtight container for up to 7 days.

Put the ricotta, milk, sugar, lime zest and egg yolks in a bowl and whisk until smooth. Fold in the flour and baking powder until just combined – overworking the batter will make it heavy.

Meanwhile, in a clean bowl whisk the egg whites to stiff peaks, then fold into the batter.

Place a large non-stick frying pan (skillet) over a medium heat and once hot, swirl around a knob of butter. Spoon a few heaped tablespoons of the batter at a time into the pan and cook for 2–3 minutes before turning carefully with a palette knife. The pancakes are a little fragile, so treat them gently – not crowding the pan will make them easier to flip. Cook for a few minutes on the other side until springy to the touch.

Serve with dollops of Greek yoghurt and the jam or your favourite pancake toppings, keeping the pancakes warm as you cook them in the unlikely event that they don't get snaffled up at once.

BANANA & CHOCOLATE CORNBREAD

A sticky, squidgy, thoroughly more-ish breakfast bread-cake, which is a little like a souped-up, Mexican-style, pain-au-chocolat. It is a great excuse for using up any bananas that are getting too ripe. You may well find yourself buying more bananas especially.

SERVES 14

80g (3oz) butter, melted, plus extra to grease

50g (2oz) Demerara sugar

300g (10½oz) ripe bananas, peeled and mashed

100ml (3½fl oz) whole milk

240g (8½oz) plain yoghurt (or buttermilk)

3 eggs

150g (5oz) unrefined or golden caster sugar

100g (3½oz) white spelt flour

150g (5oz) quick-cook polenta

1½ tsp fine salt

1 tbsp baking powder

1 tsp ground cinnamon

100g (3½oz) dark (bittersweet) chocolate (go for your favourite 70%), roughly chopped

Preheat the oven to 180°C/160°C fan/350°F/gas 4 and grease a square 20cm (8 inch) brownie tin or a 900g (2lb) loaf tin with melted butter. Add the Demerara to the tin and gently tip it so that it coats the sides and bottom.

Whisk together the bananas, milk, yoghurt and eggs in a large bowl.

In a separate bowl, combine the dry ingredients and the chocolate and deftly and briefly stir this mixture into the wet mix, along with the melted butter. Turn out into the prepared baking tin and bake for 45 minutes or until a skewer inserted into the centre comes out clean. Remove from the oven, allow to cool in the tin for 30 minutes and then turn out to slice.

This is extremely delicious with Greek yoghurt for breakfast or tea and stored in an airtight container will keep for several days, but is best toasted after day one.

SNACKS & SIDES

A little bit of this, a little bit of that. A jumble of this, a tumble of that. Cooking for and feeding friends is not the prim, starched affair of yesteryear, thank goodness. These days life is busy and time is pushed. An invitation to have dinner with friends should delight even the most jaded – real home cooking done by someone else – a total treat!!!

Do what I do and get your guests to sing for their supper. With a drink in hand and some great nibbles, most people I know are thrilled to feel useful (this wise observation on the human condition was made by Aristotle many moons ago). So, get your mates to de-stalk herbs, grate cheese, chop vegetables or make a dressing, to your careful instruction (they will want to do it well, after all), and the party will be all the more fun.

Pull together a bowl of pumpkin seed dip, Oaxacan-style spiced nuts, a plate of crispy sweetcorn nuggets or some home-made nachos with little effort; the thought and taste will wow your friends. Casually serve a plate of courgette flowers on toast or some crispy purple sprouting broccoli while you all gather round and chat, and you will have made them the chicest of starters, winning them over before they have even sat down.

However, this chapter is not just full of fancy snacks. There is a handful of mouthwatering sides that will make any other food come alive. The baked sweet potatoes with tamarind, coconut and lime are a year-round wonder and I fall back on the crispy new potatoes throughout the summer.

Cook them, taste them and make them again and again.

SMOKY SPICED NUTS
WITH FRESH LIME

These nuts, inspired by the classic bar nuts found across Oaxaca and Veracruz, are smoky, lightly drenched in aromatic spices and dressed with fresh lime, giving them a spark of exceptionally pleasing sour. They make a great start to any party, with a promising nod to what might follow (if you make a nut this good...). They disappear fast, so this recipe makes enough for both a party and a private stash. I find them an exceptionally good thing to have on any journey or adventure, nuts being such an all-round brilliant snack.

MAKES 2 BOWLS (VO)

250g (9oz) cashew nuts

250g (9oz) skin-on almonds

2 garlic cloves

1 tbsp fennel seeds

1½ tbsp cumin seeds

1–2 tsp chilli (hot pepper) flakes (pages 14 and 17)

1 tsp sweet smoked paprika

3 tbsp sunflower oil

juice of 1 lime

3 tsp flaky sea salt

2 tsp golden caster (superfine) sugar

Preheat the oven to 190°C/170°C fan/375°F/gas 5.

Empty the cashew and almond nuts onto two separate baking (cookie) sheets and put in the oven for 10 minutes, stirring them around once halfway through so as not to burn any outliers.

Meanwhile, grind the garlic and spices together in a pestle and mortar and stir in the oil.

Once the nuts have done their 10 minutes, remove from the oven and stir in the garlicky oil. Pop them back in the oven and roast the cashews for another 10–12 minutes until they are a pale caramel colour and 4–5 minutes more for the almonds. You can always taste a nut to check that it is cooked to your liking.

The second they are out of the oven, squeeze over the lime juice, sprinkle with the salt and sugar and stir well. As the nuts cool, the juice and oil will be absorbed. These are exceedingly good with a cold beer or a sparkling shrub (page 210).

COOK'S NOTE Traditionally, bar nuts like this would be laced with a few crumbled árbol chillies, but I love to scatter them with a milder, sweeter chilli like the Urfa or Ancho chilli flakes found in larger supermarkets (pages 14 and 17).

A TRIO OF GUACAMOLES

Guacamole is an avocado sauce (from the Nahuatl *molli*, meaning 'sauce', and *aguacate*, meaning 'avocado'). It is made differently wherever you go in Mexico, with some for garlic and others vehemently against; some pro fruit (tomatoes, peach, mango, pomegranate seeds), others anti. In some cities, guacamole is puréed to a thin sauce, while in others it is a chunky dip.

What is clear is that as the global demand for avocados has rocketed, so too has their price, meaning that many local cooks now mix theirs with other ingredients like nuts, peas and other pulses to make them more affordable. Not a bad idea, given how much water avocado crops need to grow in a country already experiencing droughts. So, get experimenting and see how you like yours. The Garlicky Bean Mash on page 122 makes a great dip too.

ALL RECIPES SERVE 4

THE CLASSIC

½ red onion, very finely chopped

1–2 fresh chillies, finely chopped

1–2 tsp sea salt

2 ripe large Hass avocados

juice of 1–2 limes

small handful of coriander (cilantro), chopped

plenty of freshly ground black pepper

OPTIONAL EXTRAS

1 small garlic clove

1 very ripe tomato, de-seeded and diced

Put half the onion, half the chilli and 1 teaspoon of sea salt in a pestle and mortar or a large bowl and mash to a rough paste (add the garlic here if using). Remove the avocado stones and scoop out the flesh into the pestle. Roughly mash the flesh into the chilli-salt purée with a fork, adding half the lime juice as you do. When you have a rough guacamole, stir in the rest of the lime juice, chilli, red onion and the coriander and tomato, if using. Season with plenty of black pepper and taste, adjusting the salt, chilli and fresh lime balance.

Serve with fresh tortilla chips.

MANGO & HABANERO GUACAMOLE

Weigh the flesh of 1 large Hass avocado. Weigh out an equal quantity of mango flesh. Dice the mango and mash the avocado. For every 100g (3½oz) of avocado, mix in the juice of a lime, 15g (½oz) diced red onion, a few tbsp finely chopped coriander (cilantro) stalks, ½ finely diced Scotch bonnet, dried habanero or red bullet chilli and a few tsp good olive oil. Season well, stir in the mango and serve.

PEA GUACAMOLE

Weigh the flesh of 1 large Hass avocado. Simmer an equal weight of peas in boiling water for a minute, then refresh in cold water. Mash with the avocado, then add lime, red onion, chopped green chilli and coriander (cilantro) to taste and serve as you would a classic guacamole.

SPICY PUMPKIN SEED DIP

This spicy, beautifully nuanced-tasting pumpkin seed dip is inspired by *sikil pak*, often served in kitchens in the Yucatan. It makes a delicious and healthy dip for tortilla chips and is packed with protein from the seeds. It is simple to make and its flavour only improves with age. Thin it down and drizzle over grilled asparagus, broccoli or tlayudas (page 178). If you don't have all the ingredients, just experiment with what you have. You will need a powerful blender.

MAKES A SMALL BOWL (VO)

- 150g (5oz) pumpkin seeds
- 4–6 árbol chillies (see below), to taste
- 2 tsp cumin seeds
- ½ cinnamon stick (or 1 tsp ground cinnamon)
- 1 tsp fennel seeds and/or 1 tsp hoja santa or Mexican oregano
- 3 large ripe tomatoes
- 5 large garlic cloves, unpeeled
- 1 red onion, cut into wedges
- 4 tbsp cider vinegar
- 4 tbsp rapeseed (canola) or olive oil
- 1 tsp sea salt

Toast the pumpkin seeds in a dry frying pan (skillet) over a medium heat for 8–10 minutes until most have 'popped' and are golden. Transfer them to a powerful upright blender and blitz for 2–3 minutes to a fine powder.

Toast the chillies in the same pan for 20–30 seconds a side until smelling fragrant and nutty – if they burn, they will taste bitter (page 244). Empty into the blender. Keeping the pan hot, toast the cumin, cinnamon and fennel seeds for a few minutes and transfer to the blender with the hoja santa or oregano. Whizz the lot for a minute.

Now put the tomatoes, garlic and onion into the frying pan, turn up the heat and dry roast, turning occasionally. The garlic and chilli will blacken and cook in 8–10 minutes. Remove these, peel the garlic, de-stem the chilli and transfer to the blender. The onion and tomatoes will take a further 6–8 minutes and should be blackened all over – this will make all the difference to the taste. Add to the blender with the vinegar and 3 tablespoons of the oil and blitz for at least 5 minutes, loosening with a few tablespoons of water and adding a teaspoon of sea salt.

Once you have a smooth paste, put the remaining oil into a medium saucepan and cook the paste over a medium heat for 10–15 minutes, stirring frequently. Taste – you may need a touch more salt or vinegar to sharpen the flavours. The salsa will last for several weeks in the fridge.

Serve with tortilla chips, on nachos, or as a dip for Sweetcorn Nuggets (page 70) or Grilled Asparagus (page 106) or Griddled Leeks (page 102).

COOK'S NOTE If you don't have any árbol chillies, try substituting in 2 dried habanero instead of the árbol or 2 dry-roasted Scotch bonnets.

BEETROOT, CUMIN & WALNUT DIP

This richly flavoured, deep-violet dip is inspired by some of the simpler moles I have discovered in restaurants in Mexico over the past few years. There is a saying in Mexico, '*No es mole, si no hay ajonjoli*' (it's not a real mole if it doesn't have sesame seeds), hence the addition of the tahini. It is wonderful with crudités, but I also use it as an unusual, brightly coloured base for the tlayudas on page 178.

SERVES 4 (vo)

3–4 medium beetroot (beets)

2 tbsp good olive oil, plus extra for coating

75g (2½oz) walnuts

1 green chilli

2 garlic cloves

1 tsp allspice

2 tsp cumin seeds

1 tbsp tahini

1–2 tbsp cider vinegar, to taste

salt and pepper

Preheat the oven to 200°C/180°C fan/400°F/gas 6.

Rub the beetroot with a little oil, season and wrap in foil. Roast in the oven for 50–60 minutes until tender when pierced with a knife. Allow to cool a little and then don a pair of rubber gloves and rub away the skin, using a paring knife to help if necessary.

Meanwhile, toast the walnuts on a baking tray in the same oven for 6–8 minutes until golden.

While this is happening, dry-toast the chilli and garlic in a dry frying pan (skillet) over a medium–high heat for 7–10 minutes until charred all over (page 244). Slip the skins from the garlic and de-stem the chilli (you can also de-seed it if you want a milder dip). Using the same pan, toast the allspice and cumin gently for a few minutes to release their flavour and then grind with a pestle and mortar.

Blitz the walnuts in a food processor and add the spices, garlic and chilli. Blitz again. Now add the beetroot and blitz with the engine running for a minute or two. Season generously with salt and pepper and add the tahini, a tablespoon of vinegar and the olive oil. Whizz for another minute, then taste and adjust the seasoning with more salt or vinegar. It should taste sweet and gently spiced with a delicate, rounded sharpness from the vinegar and a lovely mellow heat.

This makes a fantastic dip and a lovely addition to a mezze plate, wonderful smeared onto toast with fresh goat's cheese or curd or astride a grilled tlayuda with fresh peas, mint, ricotta and chilli oil.

IMAGE OPPOSITE: Mango & Habanero Guacamole (page 62), Spicy Pumpkin Seed Dip (page 63) and Beetroot, Cumin & Walnut Dip.

BAKED FETA & PICKLED CHILLI NACHOS

For years we didn't make nachos at Wahaca because we were so keen to showcase real Mexican food, which we felt had been hidden behind Tex-Mex for too long. Then I ate some crab nachos at Breddos Tacos that instantly converted me – we have been making nachos ever since. I first tried this recipe when I had some leftover feta, which I baked and layered with unctuous black beans, citrussy pickled onions and a beautifully sharp and fiery-as-you-want tomatillo salsa.

SERVES 4–6

Cooked Black Beans (page 75)

300g (10oz) corn tortillas (page 246) or good-quality plain tortilla chips

vegetable oil, for frying

Pink Pickled Onions (page 238)

6 radishes, finely sliced

Fresh Tomato Pico (page 226)

sour cream (optional)

FOR THE FETA

200g (7oz) feta

2 garlic cloves, finely chopped

1 tsp Mexican oregano (or some fresh thyme)

zest and juice of 1 lime

1 tsp finely chopped cascabel, ancho or other chilli (hot pepper) flakes (pages 14 and 17)

100ml (3½fl oz) extra-virgin olive oil

Preheat the oven to 220°C/200°C fan/425°F/gas 7.

Make the beans according to the recipe on page 75, using 2 tins of black beans.

Meanwhile, cut the tortillas into quarters or large triangles. Pour 2cm (¾ inch) of vegetable oil into a wide, deep frying pan (skillet) and stir-fry the chips until crisp and golden (they will crisp more after cooking). Drain on kitchen paper.

Now, drain and lay out the feta in an earthenware bowl wide enough to hold it in a single layer. Sprinkle the garlic over the feta with the herbs, lime zest and juice and the chilli. Pour over the olive oil and bake for 10–12 minutes until the cheese is creamy and soft. Be mindful that the feta will harden as it cools, so bake it at the last minute.

Lay out the warm tortilla chips and scatter with the warm black beans, pink pickled onions, radishes, tomato pico and the baked feta scattered over prettily. If you like, drizzle with sour cream. Serve at once.

ALTERNATIVE

VEGAN NACHOS WITH CHEEZ SAUCE

Put 200g (7oz) vegan cheese with 140ml (5fl oz) amber lager, water or plant-based milk in a pan. Add 1–2 tbsp Chipotles en Adobo (page 234), 1 tsp mustard powder, a dash of vegan Worcestershire sauce and 1 tsp cider vinegar. Whisk over a low heat. Roast 400g (14oz) cherry tomatoes in a hot oven with 2 tbsp olive oil and 2 tsp balsamic vinegar. Warm tortilla chips in the oven for the last 5 minutes and top with the cheese sauce, Whole Black Beans (page 75), Pumpkin Seed Salsa (page 150) and Pink Pickled Onions (page 238).

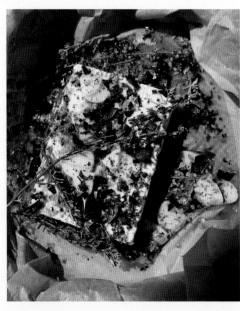

STUFFED COURGETTE FLOWERS ON TOAST

Courgette flowers were always prohibitively expensive to buy in the UK, but so many people are now growing them that they are more affordable, and prolific if you grow your own. Courgettes and pumpkins are native to Mexico, so the flowers are cheap and abundant there and used in many recipes, as are the flowers of many other edible plant species. To try to capture some of the flavours of the wonderful-tasting wild herbs in Mexico, I mix a bundle of soft herbs into the curd for a heady, evocative taste. A delicious little starter or light lunch to make for friends at the height of summer.

SERVES 6 AS A SNACK OR STARTER, LESS IF A LIGHT LUNCH

6 courgette (zucchini) flowers

2 tbsp agave syrup

2 tsp chipotle paste

2 tbsp extra-virgin olive oil, plus more for drizzling

6 slices sourdough bread, toasted on a griddle

FOR THE FILLING

120g (4½oz) shallots or sweet onions, finely chopped

2 garlic cloves, finely chopped, plus extra for the sourdough

2 tbsp extra-virgin olive oil

125g (4½oz) goat's curd or ricotta

zest and juice of ½ lemon

large handful of soft herbs (I like to mix 2–3 of parsley, chives, mint, tarragon, chervil or basil), finely chopped

salt and pepper

Gently fry the shallots and garlic in the olive oil for 8–10 minutes, seasoning well with salt and pepper. Once soft and translucent, leave to cool.

Mix the goat's curd with the lemon zest and juice, shallots, garlic and chopped herbs (reserving a small amount to garnish) and taste to check the seasoning.

Prepare the courgette flowers by removing the stamens from the centre. Gently spoon the filling into the flowers, aiming for a generous tablespoon in each, although this will vary if you have smaller flowers. Fold the petals very carefully to close and secure the filling by twisting the ends around. You can refrigerate them at this stage, but allow them to come to room temperature before sautéing them.

Mix the agave syrup and the chipotle in a pan on a low heat, stirring to combine and tasting to see if you would like more chipotle for more smoky heat.

Heat the oil in a pan and cook the flowers over a medium–high heat. Depending on the pan size, you may need to do this in 2–3 batches, cooking the flowers for roughly 2 minutes each side and turning them gently to keep the filling intact.

Rub each slice of toasted sourdough with garlic, drizzle with a little olive oil, and then top with a courgette flower, a generous drizzle of the chipotle agave and a sprinkle of herbs.

CRISPY SWEETCORN NUGGETS

WITH SWEET CHILLI SAUCE

These deep-fried, crispy sweetcorn nuggets are totally delicious and dairy-free, making them a great starter for those on a plant-based diet. I love to serve them with crème fraîche and a home-made salsa or a spoonful of smoky harissa. A brilliant bite for a party on a balmy summer's evening.

MAKES 18–20 NUGGETS (VO)

360g (13oz) sweetcorn (from approx. 3 cobs)

1½ tsp baking powder

6 spring onions (scallions), finely chopped

30g (1oz) Chipotles en Adobo (page 234), chopped

3 garlic cloves, crushed

30g (1oz) coriander (cilantro) leaves, finely chopped

juice of 2 limes (3 tbsp)

120g (4½oz) chickpea (gram) flour

1½ tsp ground cumin

1 tsp allspice

1 tsp brown sugar

rapeseed (canola) oil, for frying

salt and pepper

TO SERVE

crème fraîche or vegan crème fraîche alternative

Salsa Negra (page 226), Salsa Macha (page 237) or smoked harissa paste

coriander (cilantro) leaves

Cut the corn from their cobs using a sharp chopping knife. Place half the sweetcorn in a food processor and blitz for 20–30 seconds. Mix this with the rest of the corn in a large bowl.

Add the rest of the ingredients apart from the oil and season generously with salt and pepper. You will need at least 1 teaspoon of sea salt.

Pour enough oil into a pan or wok so that it is at least 5–7cm (2–3 inches) deep. Bring to a temperature of 160–180°C (320–350°F). Test a little of the mixture – it should sizzle and start to brown in 20–30 seconds; if it burns or cooks too quickly, turn the heat down and allow the oil to cool for a few minutes.

Shape spoonfuls of the mixture and fry in batches of 5–6 depending on the size of your pan. Fry for about 2 minutes until pale golden all over. Serve with the crème fraîche, salsa or harissa paste and a sprinkle of coriander leaves.

BROCCOLI TEMPURA

WITH SMOKY RED MAYO
& LIME-SOY DIPPING SAUCE

A recipe for setting the room alight. There is a love affair for all things Japanese in Mexico and once you have tasted the marriage of jalapeño, soy and lime you will find it amazing that you never put those flavours together before. It makes a more-ish seasoning for the feather-light batter encasing the broccoli. The mayo adds a layer of smoky warmth to dip the sticks into. Get everything prepped before and then effortlessly present plates of this. Fun and deliriously delicious.

SERVES 4–6 (vo)

400g (14oz) purple sprouting or Tenderstem broccoli, any tough stems discarded

50g (2oz) cornflour (cornstarch)

150g (5oz) plain (all-purpose) or white spelt flour

1 tsp baking powder

250ml (8fl oz) ice-cold sparkling water

rapeseed (canola) oil, for frying

1 tsp sea salt

1 lime, cut into wedges

Smoky Chipotle Mayo (page 240 – or use vegan mayo)

FOR THE DIPPING SAUCE

½–1 Thai green chilli, serrano or jalapeño

2 tbsp lime juice

3 tbsp good-quality light soy sauce

If you have purple sprouting broccoli, you will need to peel the stalks and cut them into thinner batons so that they cook evenly. I usually divide thicker stalks into quarters along their lengths.

Make the dipping sauce first. Put the chilli in a pan over a high heat and dry toast it (page 244). Once blackened all over, pound in a pestle and mortar with the lime juice. Stir in the soy sauce and taste – it should have a rich, rounded flavour with a light brush of heat. You can add more chilli if you would like but remember the aioli is spicy too. Set aside.

Make the batter by sifting the flours and baking powder together in a large bowl and slowly whisking in the sparkling water; you want it to be the consistency of thick but pourable cream. Add extra water or flour if needed.

In a deep pan or wok, add the oil to a depth of about 4cm (1½ inches) and heat it to about 180°C (350°F) – test the temperature by dropping in a bit of bread; if it turns golden in 30 seconds, the oil is the right temperature, or use a cooking thermometer.

Dip the broccoli in the batter and shake off any excess. Carefully lower into the hot oil and fry until the batter is crisp and golden, about 2–3 minutes. Don't crowd the pan – you will need to do this in batches. Remove and drain on kitchen paper. Serve with the dipping sauce and mayo.

ALTERNATIVE

CRISPY CAULIFLOWER WITH JALAPEÑO AIOLI

To make the incredibly popular crispy cauliflower we serve at Wahaca, use cauliflower florets instead and serve with the jalapeño aioli on page 240.

CARROT & CORIANDER FRITTERS

These are so simple to make, with such easy ingredients, that I find myself turning to them time and again for a fun starter, or a light snack or lunch for the children and me. They are totally delicious with coriander salsa, or try them stuffed inside a taco with the charred Spring Onion Crema on page 242 and some baby kale. Do give them a go, I promise you won't be disappointed.

MAKES 12–14 FRITTERS

500g (1lb 2oz) carrots, peeled and grated

1 small red onion (about 100g/3½oz), finely chopped

1 tsp cumin seeds

1 tsp allspice berries

1 tsp sweet paprika

2 tsp salt

2 eggs

½ tsp baking powder

80g (3oz) chickpea (gram) flour

2–3 tbsp finely chopped coriander (cilantro) stalks

rapeseed (canola) oil, for frying

TO SERVE

sour cream, crème fraîche or Cashew Nut 'Crema' (page 242)

Quick Coriander Chimichurri Salsa (page 235)

Put the carrot and onion into a bowl. Toast the cumin and allspice for a few minutes in a dry frying pan (skillet), then grind to a powder in a pestle and mortar. Add to the carrot with the paprika, salt and eggs and mix well. At this stage you could make the salsa.

When you are ready to eat, warm a large frying pan over a medium–high heat. Sift the baking powder and chickpea flour over the carrot, add the coriander stalks and mix in well. Add 1 tablespoon of oil to the pan and swirl around. Add tablespoons of the carrot mixture to the pan and smooth down with the back of a spoon. Fry for a few minutes on each side until golden, then transfer to a plate and keep warm in the oven while you cook the rest, adding more oil for each batch and when the pan looks dry.

Serve with dollops of sour cream, crème fraîche or Cashew Nut 'Crema' and the Coriander Chimichurri Salsa. If you want to make this into a more substantial lunch, serve with grilled halloumi, the closest thing you can get to the panela cheese in Mexico.

COOK'S NOTE To make these vegan, take out the eggs and instead mix in 2 tablespoons of flaxseeds previously soaked with 6 tablespoons of cold water.

SNACKS & SIDES

WHOLE BLACK BEANS & TWICE-COOKED BEANS

Beans, the ultimate superfood – they are uniquely rich in both protein and fibre. Of all the Mexican varieties, black beans are said to be the most nutritious.

WHOLE BLACK BEANS

An ever-useful recipe for cooking beans from scratch. Substitute in any dried bean, whether pinto, flor de mayo or any other you might find.

SERVES 4–6

250g (9oz) dried black turtle beans

4 fat garlic cloves

few bay leaves

1 star anise, a few avocado leaves or a large pinch of epazote or hoja santa

½ white onion, peeled

1 tsp bicarbonate of soda (baking soda)

1 large tsp salt

Soak the beans overnight or see page 247 for a great hack for cooking beans fast from dried.

After soaking, place the beans in a large pan and cover with at least 10cm (4 inches) of cold water. Smash the garlic cloves with the flat side of a knife and add to the beans with the herbs, aromatics, onion and bicarbonate of soda. Bring to the boil and cook until just soft, 1–2 hours depending on the age of the beans, skimming off any white foam that gathers on the surface. Season with the salt when the beans are starting to soften, about 1 hour into the cooking time.

Serve in Cheesy Brunch Burritos (page 45), Cauliflower Tacos (page 93), scatter over nachos (page 66), use to fill quesadillas (pages 104–5), or serve as a delicious side topped with a little sprinkled Lancashire cheese, feta or Crema (page 242).

TWICE-COOKED BEANS

Comfort food packed with protein and fibre. In Mexico they are called *refrito*, meaning 'well fried', when twice-cooked like this and this is the key. Cook them slowly and you will taste their magic.

SERVES 4–6

3 tbsp olive oil or 45g (1½oz) butter

1 white onion, finely chopped

2 garlic cloves, finely chopped

2 tsp Chipotles in Adobo (page 234) (optional)

2 x 400g (14oz) tins black beans or 600g (1¼lb) home-cooked beans (see left)

pinch of ground star anise (optional)

large knob of butter (optional)

salt and pepper

SERVING SUGGESTIONS

sour cream

grated Lancashire cheese or hard sheep's cheese

Heat the fat in a heavy-bottomed pan and, when gently foaming, add the onion, garlic and adobo, if using. Season well with salt and pepper and sweat gently for about 10 minutes until soft. Add the beans, star anise (if using) and 300ml (10½fl oz) water or the bean cooking liquid and cook for another 10 minutes.

Whizz into a smooth, thick purée, loosening with either the cooking liquid or some water, according to the consistency you are after. This will depend if you are using it to top nachos (loose) or as a dip for chilaquiles (not so loose). Taste and adjust the seasoning, stirring in a knob of butter if you would like them to shine.

Serve straight up or as a side, drizzled with sour cream and scattered with a little cheese.

CHIPOTLE-TAMARIND BAKED SWEET POTATO GRATIN

The smoky, sweet-sour combination of tamarind and chipotle is used throughout the eastern coastal regions of southern Mexico to anoint giant shrimp, lobster and crab, often with the addition of coconut. It is an intoxicating combination for sweet shellfish so I thought I would try it with sweet potato. It really is delightful, with tangy sour from the lime and tamarind, sweet nuttiness from the coconut and a mellow, smoky heat from the chipotle. Serve with a light green salad and, if you like, a bowl of lightly dressed lentils for something more substantial.

SERVES 6

4 tbsp tamarind paste from 80g (3oz) tamarind pods (page 245)

100g (3½oz) coconut cream

30g (1oz) Chipotles en Adobo (page 234)

4 garlic cloves, crushed

40ml (1½fl oz) lime juice

50ml (2fl oz) olive oil

1kg (2¼lb) sweet potatoes, sliced into 2–3mm (⅛ inch) rounds

2 red onions

large handful of coriander (cilantro), finely chopped

1 lime, sliced into rounds

150ml (5fl oz) vegetable stock

Preheat the oven to 220°C/200°C fan/425°F/gas 7. You will need a wide, round ovenproof dish, approx. 12–13cm (5 inches) diameter.

Prepare the tamarind paste following the instructions on page 245. To the paste add the coconut cream, chipotle, garlic, lime juice and olive oil and put over a low heat to melt the cream. Meanwhile, briefly scrub the sweet potatoes under cold water to remove any grit and only peel them if they don't look clean. Slice into thin rounds – using a mandolin will make this much quicker, just try not to cut yourself! Cut the onions in half, peel and thinly slice too.

Toss the coriander and all but 2 tablespoons of the tamarind-chipotle glaze with the potato and onion. Season the lot with plenty of salt and pepper and arrange the slices upright in a spiral in the baking dish, squeezing in the red onion and lime slices between the sweet potato slices (to ensure maximum caramelisation).

Pour in the stock and bake, covered with foil, for 45 minutes. Remove the foil and cook for a further 20–25 minutes, brushing with the remaining glaze, until the top is caramelised, golden and crispy.

ALTERNATIVE

SWEET POTATO CHUNKS AL AJILLO

One of the most popular dishes at Wahaca is our crispy sweet potato chunks. My home version is to cut 3 sweet potatoes into rough cubes and toss in 150ml (5fl oz) Ajillo Oil (page 236) and fresh thyme OR an olive oil paste made up of 150ml (5fl oz) olive oil, 4 garlic cloves, thyme and chipotle or smoked pimentón. Roast in an extremely hot oven for 40–45 minutes until caramelised and dark in patches. Serve as a side or as an outrageously good nibble, with the jalapeño aioli on page 240.

GRILLED CORN ON THE COB, MEXICAN-STYLE

Make one of these per person and a few more for luck – they disappear as fast as you dress them up with their mouthwatering toppings. I often cook them inside on my griddle pan, but they are at their most tantalising when they are cooked over an open fire. They make a brilliant addition to any late-summer spread.

MAKES 4 (vo)

- 4 corn on the cobs
- 4 tbsp extra-virgin olive oil
- Chilli-lime-salt (page 132)

Peel back the sleeves of the corn and remove the strands of silk clinging to the husks. Cover the husks with the sleeves again and soak in cold water for 15–20 minutes or overnight.

Heat the barbecue, if using.

When the barbecue is hot, put the still-wrapped cobs straight onto the barbecue grills and turn them for 10–15 minutes until the husks blacken and become like tissue paper.

Alternatively, brush them with oil and cook them on a griddle pan, using the peeled-back leaves as handles, or bake them, peeled and oiled, in an oven preheated to 220°C/200°C fan/425°F/gas 7 for 15–20 minutes, then dress with one of the toppings below.

TOPPINGS

HABANERO MAYO, CHILLI-LIME-SALT

Smear with Habanero Mayo (page 240) and sprinkle with Chilli-lime-salt (page 132). A crumble of feta is delicious.

CHIPOTLE MAYO, PECORINO, CORIANDER

Lather in Smoky Chipotle Mayo (page 240), scatter in a cloud of Microplaned vegetarian pecorino or hard goat's cheese and dust in chilli powder and fresh coriander (cilantro).

CHIPOTLE BUTTER, FETA, FRESH LIME

Mash up 2 tbsp Chipotles en Adobo (page 235) with 100g (3½oz) butter and smear all over the corn once it has cooked. Crumble over some feta and squeeze over a lime. The smoky fieriness of the chillies and the sweet grilled corn are the definition of finger-licking.

CHEDDAR CHEESE & PICKLED JALAPEÑO SCONES

I love to make these wickedly crumbly scones for breakfast or tea, spread with butter that melts into the soft, light crumb, topped with a fresh young goat's cheese (hello White Lake Farm), although a mild cows' cheese or curd works well too. Spoon over heaped teaspoons of the iridescent tomato jam and revel in the bursts of flavour from the pickled chillies and Demerara crust. It is a fine way to start the day and an easy way to win over friends. Throw a brunch party, bake these, sip some strong coffee followed by a few bellinis. My idea of a good weekend.

MAKES 8 LARGE SCONES

340g (12oz) self-raising flour, plus extra for dusting

few pinches of salt

1½ tsp baking powder

100g (3½oz) butter, chilled and cut into cubes

220g (8oz) mature Cheddar cheese, grated (or any mix of cheeses you have left in the fridge)

130–150ml (4½–5fl oz) whole milk, plus 1 tbsp for glazing

30–40g (1–1½oz) green pickled chillies, roughly chopped

30–40g (1–1½oz) Demerara sugar

TO SERVE

butter

goat's curd or cheese

Sweet Tomato Chilli Jam (page 233)

Preheat the oven to 200°C/180°C fan/400°F/gas 6 with a large baking tray inside.

Sift the flour, salt and baking powder into a large mixing bowl. Add the butter and lightly and deftly rub it in with your fingertips to make breadcrumbs. Sprinkle 120g (4½oz) of the cheese into the flour and butter mixture and briefly mix through.

Make a well in the centre of the mixture, pour in two-thirds of the milk and the chillies, and lightly mix in with a fork first, followed by your hands. Then add just enough milk for the mixture to come together, mixing as lightly and little as possible for a feather-light scone. Do not worry if it isn't perfectly smooth, as long as you can roughly hold it together.

Lightly flour a surface and shape the dough into a rough 12cm (4½ inch) round that's 3–4cm (1¼–1½ inch) thick. Cut the scones into eight slices like a pizza, brush with the extra milk and sprinkle with the remaining cheese and the Demerara sugar. Slide onto the hot oven tray.

Bake in the oven for 20–25 minutes or until golden brown and cooked through. Cool on a wire rack for 10 minutes before slicing open and slathering in butter, goat's cheese and the tomato jam.

A TRIO OF RICE

This trio of rice follows the tradition of making rice in the three colours of the Mexican flag but with a fresh take on the recipes. Finding time to soak the rice for 15–20 minutes before cooking gives a light, beautifully textured rice, but if you are cooking on the fly, as is so often the case, rinse it a few times in cold water instead and don't use too much water. Then just leave the rice for a final 15–20 minutes, 'fluffing' in a warm place to allow the rice grains to steam. It is the tried-and-tested method of most Mexican grannies and it allows you to get ahead, leaving the rice for a few hours in a low oven or warming drawer, covered well. Alternatively, you can stop midway and do the final 'fluff' in the microwave just before eating. Either way, you will get a tender kernel, full of flavour and texture. Use any of these in the Mexican bowls on pages 126–127. They also make a great lunch topped with avocado slices, some greens, a fried or poached egg, a dollop of any salsa, sesame seeds, spring onions and coriander leaves.

ALL RECIPES SERVE 4

WHITE RICE WITH PUMPKIN SEEDS & FRESH LIME

A blissfully simple, sophisticated rice.

2 tbsp sesame oil

2 tbsp vegetable oil

2–3 garlic cloves, chopped

300g (10oz) short-grain rice, rinsed

1½ tbsp soy sauce

juice of 1 lime

salt

FOR THE MIXED SEEDS

100g (3½oz) pumpkin seeds

40g (1½oz) sesame seeds

1 tbsp soy sauce

1 tsp ground cumin

SERVING SUGGESTIONS

finely sliced jalapeño

coriander (cilantro) leaves

finely chopped spring onions (scallions)

Warm 1 tablespoon of the sesame oil and the vegetable oil in a medium pan over a medium heat and when warm, add the garlic and several pinches of salt. Cook for a few minutes, then add the rice and cook for another few minutes, just until the rice begins to turn translucent but before the garlic has darkened.

Add 700ml (24fl oz) hot water and the soy sauce, bring to the boil and then turn the heat down and cover. Simmer gently for 25 minutes, squeeze over the lime juice, then take off the heat, cover and leave to sit for 30 minutes. If needed, add 2 tablespoons of hot water and steam over a low heat for a final 5 minutes. Toast the seeds in a dry frying pan until 'popping', then stir in the soy and cumin for a few minutes.

Put the rice in a serving bowl and sprinkle over the rest of the sesame oil, some mixed seeds and the jalapeño, coriander and spring onions.

COOK'S NOTE Most rice is grown in flooded paddy fields and it is responsible for 12% of global methane emissions. Experiments with growing new varieties of rice from seed have been hugely successful and are virtually methane free, so keep your eyes out for seed-grown rice, the green rice of the future!

GREEN RICE WITH CORIANDER & SPINACH

This rice is served all over Mexico and is always on our menus at Wahaca. Its delicate flavour goes beautifully with fish or chicken, while its wonderful emerald-green colour makes a pretty addition to any table.

300g (10oz) long-grain rice, rinsed

2 garlic cloves

1 small white onion

large handful of coriander (cilantro)

large bunch of parsley

100g (3½oz) spinach

2 tbsp olive oil

salt and pepper

Cover the rice in 500ml (17fl oz) water, season well with salt and pepper and cook for about 20 minutes until the rice is nearly tender. Meanwhile, whizz the garlic, onion, herbs and spinach in a food processor with a splash of water until you have a thick green purée.

Heat the oil in a wide pan and when warm, add the purée and stir-fry for a few minutes over a medium heat to cook out the raw onion. Add to the rice and stir well to combine. Cook for another few minutes until most of the liquid has been absorbed, before covering with butter papers or parchment paper and a lid. Transfer to a low oven for 15–20 minutes and keep warm until you are ready to eat.

RED RICE WITH SUN-DRIED TOMATO & SESAME

Inspired by a work trip to Chicago in 2015, this umami-rich red rice is served in DF Tacos and is a brilliant addition to a taco bowl (page 126). I can eat an entire bowl of this standing up.

1½ tbsp olive or rapeseed (canola) oil

300g (10oz) long-grain rice, rinsed

50g (2oz) sun-dried tomatoes

50g (2oz) tomato purée

1 garlic clove, roughly chopped

4 spring onions (scallions), roughly chopped

10g (½oz) ginger, chopped

2 tsp brown sugar

3 tbsp light soy sauce

1 tbsp sesame oil

1–2 tsp Chipotles en Adobo (page 234) (optional)

1 tsp salt

In a wide pan set over a medium heat, warm the oil and when hot, add the rice. Fry, stirring, for 3–4 minutes until evenly golden and smelling toasty.

Meanwhile, place the remaining ingredients in a blender or small food processor. When the rice is looking ready, turn the heat down, pour in the paste (careful, it'll spit) and stir for 3–4 minutes to darken and give it a chance to be absorbed, then pour over 600ml (21fl oz) water.

Stir well, then reduce the heat to low and simmer gently for 15 minutes. Now put somewhere warm or turn the heat to its lowest setting and cover. Leave to steam-cook for a minimum of 15 minutes or leave in a warm oven/drawer for anything up to 2–3 hours.

Serve as per the white rice opposite.

CRISPY NEW POTATOES

WITH GARLIC, ÁRBOL & THYME

A simple yet delicious side of new potatoes that is a wonderful accompaniment to any griddled or barbecued food through the summer.

SERVES 4 (VO)

1kg (2½lb) Jersey Royals (baby potatoes)

2 heads of garlic, broken into cloves

1 tbsp thyme leaves

2 árbol chillies, cut into small pieces with scissors

1½ tsp cumin seeds

2 tsp coriander seeds

7 tbsp olive oil

salt and pepper

Preheat the oven to 200°C/180°C fan/400°F/gas 6.

Place the potatoes in a large pan of salted boiling water and cook for 15–20 minutes until tender. Drain, then leave to steam-dry for 5 minutes.

Meanwhile, combine the garlic, thyme, chillies, spices and oil in a bowl and season generously.

Transfer the potatoes to a baking tray and use the bottom of a cup to gently press down and flatten them. Tip over the garlic and oil mix and gently toss with the potatoes so they're nicely coated. Lay out on the baking tray and cook in the oven for 45–50 minutes until the potatoes are crispy and the garlic is sweet and caramelised.

TACOS & SMALLER PLATES

Antojitos. In English, you might say 'little whims'. A typically romantic name for the collection of street-food snacks served at food stands across this fantastical country. The 'tapas' are based on corn, mankind's first crop and the original superfood. The corn is picked, soaked, cooked and ground into a dough called 'masa'. With this you can make tortillas and many different street foods, which are cooked on a comal, a flat sheet of metal suspended over fired coals or wood.

What you put inside is a subject of endless fascination. You might be swayed by garlic and chilli-spiked sautéed mushrooms; courgette flowers tossed with caramelised onions or greens (called *quelites*). But Mexican cooking has long been influenced by a melting pot of countries from Japan to Italy, France to the Middle East.

So, experiment in this chapter with the 'Spanish' sautéed green bean tacos with tomato pico and toasted almonds, or the crispy tofu tacos with spring onion relish inspired by the mouth-watering mish-mash Mexican-Korean fusion in Chicago. Revel in a seasonal take on gorditas using wild garlic, or be won over by the vegetarian take on cochinita pibil using achiote-marinated roast cauliflower instead of pork or experiment with quick quesadilla fillings to please a crowd. No matter what you choose, this is a chapter full of food that can sit happily on a lunch table, as part of an exciting spread, as a starter or a satisfying supper.

BLISTERED GREEN BEAN TACOS
WITH TOMATO PICO & TOASTED ALMONDS

I had a taco stuffed with sautéed green beans several years ago in a tiny Mexican restaurant in Barcelona. It felt like such a simple idea – to stuff a warm tortilla with an ingredient that for me is so quintessentially British. I can still remember the delight I felt as a child when surreptitiously snapping them off the plants in my aunt's garden in Wales, where we would go for the summer holidays. Try this in the summer when both the green beans and the tomatoes are at their best: runner beans, griddled flat beans or sugar snaps will all taste good.

SERVES 4 (VO)

75g (2½oz) flaked (slivered) almonds

500g (1lb 2oz) green beans, topped

2 tbsp olive oil

3 garlic cloves, sliced

3 tbsp capers (the bigger the better)

12 small corn or flour tortillas (pages 245–6)

sea salt

TO SERVE

Fresh Tomato Pico (page 226)

crumbled feta (optional)

sliced avocado (optional)

Put your largest frying pan (skillet) over a medium heat and when hot, toast the almonds, shaking the pan until they are mostly a lighter shade of caramel. Put aside to cool.

Turn the heat up under the pan and add the beans in two batches. Sauté each batch for 4–5 minutes until they are looking a little blackened all over and starting to blister. Season with sea salt and remove from the pan into a warm bowl. Now pour in the olive oil and add the garlic and drained capers (watch for spitting if they are still a little wet). Cook for a couple of minutes or so until the garlic is golden and empty onto the beans.

Warm the tortillas in a pan, over a flame or in the microwave (page 245) and wrap in a dish towel to keep hot.

Pile the beans into the tortillas and top with the garlic and capers, spooning over heaped spoonfuls of the tomato salsa. Sprinkle with the almonds and crumbled feta and avocado, if using, then munch with gusto.

COOK'S NOTE I also love this with the olive oil-rich cooked tomato sauce on page 160 using ripe, summery tomatoes, or the more fiery Roast Chipotle Salsa on page 228 will also work a treat.

CRISPY TOFU TACOS
WITH BURNT SPRING ONION RELISH & SRIRACHA MAYO

Despite developing a large range of seasonal vegetarian taco recipes for Wahaca, it was not until writing this book that I started experimenting with tofu tacos in earnest and this taco came into being. Wholeheartedly inspired by the outrageously good, irreverent mix of Korean flavours and Mexican sass at the Kogi Taco Truck in LA, it has converted all three of my children to the joys of tofu.

SERVES 4 (vo)

1 tbsp honey or maple syrup

2 tbsp sriracha

100g (3½oz) fine cornmeal or fine polenta

1 tbsp each white and black sesame seeds (or 2 of one type)

1 tsp salt

6 tbsp vegetable oil, for frying

280g (10oz) firm tofu, drained, dried with kitchen paper and cut into 2cm (¾ inch) cubes

TO SERVE

Burnt Spring Onion Relish (page 238)

2 tbsp sriracha

drizzle of maple syrup

150g (5oz) mayonnaise (there are good vegan brands now)

½ red cabbage, shredded

juice of 1 lime, plus extra to serve

12 corn or flour tortillas (pages 245–6)

handful of coriander (cilantro) leaves, chopped

salt and pepper

Get all the taco ingredients ready first. Make the burnt spring onion relish. Combine the sriracha, maple syrup and mayonnaise and put to one side. Toss together the cabbage and lime juice, season lightly and put to one side.

Combine the honey or maple syrup and sriracha in one large bowl and the cornmeal, sesame seeds and salt in another.

Place a wide frying pan (skillet) or wok over a medium–high heat and add the oil. Dip the tofu cubes in the honey mix, then toss them in the cornmeal. Once the oil is hot, add a batch of the coated tofu (try not to crowd the pan) and fry, gently turning over the cubes as they turn golden, about 5–6 minutes. Use a slotted spoon to remove and drain on kitchen paper while you fry the rest. At the same time, you can be warming the tortillas in a pan (page 245), wrapping them in a dish towel to keep warm.

Make the tacos by stuffing the warm tortillas with the lime-dressed cabbage, with the crispy tofu bundled in on top with generous spoonfuls of the spring onion relish and the sriracha mayo ladled over. Uh-huh. Sprinkle with the coriander, then serve.

QUICK-ROAST CAULIFLOWER TACOS
WITH PINK PICKLED ONIONS

Achiote paste comes from the ground berries of the achiote tree, found throughout Mexico but particularly used in the Yucatán. It has a distinctive brick-red colour and a tangy, fruity flavour, which produces a sensationally quick and delicious rub for cauliflower, staining it ochre as it roasts. Serve with the pink onions and black beans, also widely cooked in the Yucatán, and you could almost be in Mérida. A mild dish which is easy to give pleasing accents of heat by lacing the pickled onions with finely chopped Scotch bonnet chilli.

SERVES 4 (vo)

70g (2½oz) achiote paste

3 large garlic cloves

1 tsp brown sugar

6 tbsp plain or plant-based yoghurt

1 tbsp lime juice

5 tbsp extra-virgin olive oil, plus extra for the cauliflower

1 tsp Mexican oregano or 2 tbsp thyme leaves

1 large head of cauliflower or 2 smaller ones

sea salt and pepper

TO SERVE

corn or flour tortillas (pages 245–6)

Pink Pickled Onions (page 238)

Cooked Black Beans (page 75)

Crema, sour cream or Cashew Nut 'Crema' (page 242) (optional)

Preheat the oven to 220°C/200°C fan/425°F/gas 7.

Smash the achiote, garlic, sugar and ½ teaspoon of salt together in a pestle and mortar to a paste. Stir in the yoghurt, lime juice, olive oil and herbs, followed by plenty of freshly ground black pepper.

Cut the florets from the stem of the cauliflower, discarding the tough outer leaves and the gnarly end of the stem, but keeping the tender inner leaves and the inner core, both of which are delicious. Cut the larger florets into halves or quarters and the inner core into chunks – you want bite-size pieces, but they will shrink with roasting.

Empty the lot onto a large roasting tray or two smaller ones – you need enough space for a single layer – and smear everything with the paste. Scrunch over a little sea salt, drizzle with a last flourish of olive oil and roast for 30–35 minutes until nicely browned and caramelised all over.

Serve with the tortillas, pickled onions, black beans and crema, letting everyone build their own tacos.

GARLIC, SOY & LIME CAULIFLOWER TACOS
WITH AVOCADO SALSA

My three children have never failed to tell me how much they hate cauliflower. Frustrating when, roasted or raw, it can be transformed into so many incredible dishes. Enter in our amazing childminder SeaSea, who regularly delights me with her imaginative flair in the kitchen. She does something so magical to cauliflower, steaming and then sautéing it in improbable amounts of soy and garlic, that my children fight over the remnants in the pan. One day, unable to hold back, I stuffed a few leftover bits inside a hot tortilla and doused it with salsa. Thus, this taco was born, and it is a delight. Go SeaSea!

MAKES 4   (vo)

1 large head of cauliflower

5 tbsp olive oil

6 garlic cloves, sliced

1 tsp grated ginger

1 tsp rice vinegar

juice of ½ lime

6 tbsp soy sauce

12 corn or flour tortillas (pages 245–6)

lime wedges, to serve

FOR THE AVOCADO SALSA

1 avocado

20g (¾oz) coriander (cilantro) leaves and stalks

3 pickled chillies

juice of 1 lime

200g (7oz) good tomatillo salsa (see Sweet Cascabel and Tomatillo Salsa on page 229)

salt and pepper

Peel away the outer leaves of the cauliflower (I compost really tough ones, feed medium-tender ones to our guinea pigs and throw younger, tender leaves into the pan with the florets) and, using a knife, break the head of the cauliflower up into florets. Steam for 6–7 minutes until just tender.

Meanwhile, make the avocado salsa by blitzing the ingredients together until smooth and seasoning to taste.

Heat the olive oil in a large pan or wok and add the cauliflower. Sauté over a medium–high heat for a few minutes and then add the garlic. Continue to cook until everything is starting to colour and smell fragrant, then add the ginger. Stir-fry for a minute, then finally add the vinegar, lime and soy sauce. Cook until the liquid has all but simmered off and the pan is almost dry.

Heat the tortillas in a frying pan (skillet) or microwave (page 245), then stuff with the cauliflower and ladle over the salsa. A squeeze of fresh lime is the only thing missing ...

ROAST AUBERGINE TACOS
WITH GOAT'S CHEESE & MINT

The smoky hibiscus salsa in this recipe is like a sophisticated ketchup, dolled up with floral notes from the hibiscus and a gentle, smoky background heat from the chipotle. Its sweetness is a great foil for the crisp roast aubergine. A fresh, young goat's cheese and shredded mint leaves are all you need to add a lightness to these otherwise sultry flavours.

SERVES 4 (VO)

3 aubergines (eggplants), cut into 2–3cm (1 inch) cubes

approx. 5 tbsp rapeseed (canola) oil

Smoky Hibiscus Salsa (page 229)

2 baby gems

handful of mint leaves

juice of ½ lemon

12 corn or flour tortillas (pages 245–6)

salt and pepper

TO SERVE

goat's cheese, crumbled

½ small red onion, very finely chopped (optional)

Preheat the oven to 220°C/200°C fan/425°F/gas 7. Line one large or two small baking trays with parchment paper.

Place the aubergine in a pile on the baking tray(s), add the oil, several pinches of salt and a few grindings of black pepper and toss well to coat. Spread out across the baking tray(s), then roast in the oven for 20 minutes. At this stage, remove them from the oven, toss in a few tablespoons of the hibiscus salsa and put them back in the oven for another 5–10 minutes until tender and crispy around the edges, but before the salsa can burn.

Tear open the baby gem leaves, wash in cold water and finely shred. Run a chopping knife through the mint leaves and add them to a bowl with the baby gem. Season lightly and toss them in a teaspoon of the lemon juice.

Warm up the tortillas in a dry pan (page 245) and wrap in a dish towel to keep warm. Gently warm the smoky hibiscus salsa in a small pan, adding enough water to loosen.

Put everything on the table, piling handfuls of the lettuce in each tortilla, followed by the aubergine and the crumbled goat's cheese and top with the salsa and a sprinkle of diced onion, if using.

ALTERNATIVE

ROAST AUBERGINE, PRESERVED LEMON & MINT TACOS

The above recipe with diced preserved lemon instead of the goat's cheese is a vegan winner.

A TRIO OF EMPANADAS

Flaky, buttery, melt-in-the-mouth pastry encasing all manner of street-food fillings. In Mexico empanadas are typically fried until puffed up and crispy, but they are also delicious when baked in the oven which involves a lot less mess, so I never do it any other way. Thought to have been influenced by the influx of Cornish miners in the nineteenth century, the state of Hidalgo is particularly famous for its 'pastes'. The dough is dead easy and can be made with vegetable oil in place of butter (you can leave out the egg or experiment with chia seeds for a dairy-free version). I have given you three rich and flavour-packed fillings to experiment with which can also be used to fill a quesadilla or top a tlayuda (page 178). They are a lovely thing to bake at the weekend, and should you have smalls in the house, are great fun to assemble.

MAKES 8–12 EMPANADAS

FOR THE PASTRY (OR USE A 250G/9OZ PACKET OF READY-MADE PUFF PASTRY)

400g (14oz) white spelt flour, chilled, plus extra for sprinkling

few good tsp of salt

165g (6oz) butter, chilled and cut into small cubes

1 egg, beaten

80–130ml (2½–4½fl oz) ice-cold water

1 egg yolk, for brushing

Put the flour and salt in a food processor and pulse a few times. Add the butter and pulse again a couple of times, but be very careful not to overwork the dough or it will become tough. Add the egg and 50ml (1¾fl oz) of the iced water and keep pulsing briefly, adding just enough water to form a clumpy dough that just comes together. Divide the dough in half, shape into balls and flatten out. Wrap and chill in the fridge for up to 2 days but at least for a few hours.

When you are ready to make the empanadas and have your cooked filling ready and cooled, preheat the oven to 200°C/180°C fan/400°F/gas 6.

Roll out the balls of dough into thin sheets and cut out round discs, around 10–12cm (4–4½ inches) in diameter OR make small balls and use a tortilla press to flatten them out.

HOW TO FOLD EMPANADAS

1 Place a spoonful of filling into the middle of each pastry disc, bearing in mind they will be much easier to seal if they are not over-filled.

2 Fold the dough over into a half-moon and seal the edges by pressing the dough between your fingers, using a little water if you need to.

3 Use a fork to crimp the edges or make a series of little folds.

4 Prick the pastry a few times with a fork, whisk the egg yolk with a little water and brush the pastries just before baking. Bake in the oven for roughly 20 minutes, or until the pastries are crisp and golden. Eat at once.

MUSHROOM, TRUFFLE & MOZZARELLA

Huitlacoche is a fungus that grows on corn with a heady truffle-like flavour. It is a much sought-after ingredient in Mexico. One year, Riverford Organic's corn harvest found some on their corn and we promptly bought the lot. As far as we know, it was the first example of anyone in the UK cooking with locally grown huitlacoche! It is available in tins from specialist suppliers or use truffle oil instead.

2–3 tbsp olive oil

1 red onion, finely diced

1 large garlic clove, crushed

1 árbol chilli, crumbled, or a pinch of chilli (hot pepper) flakes (optional)

pinch of Mexican oregano or 1–2 tbsp thyme leaves

200g (7oz) small portobello mushrooms, sliced

200g (7oz) huitlacoche or ½ tsp truffle oil

100g (3½oz) sweetcorn

200g (7oz) new potatoes, cooked and diced

100g (3½oz) mozzarella, grated

100g (3½oz) Cheddar cheese, grated

salt and pepper

Heat a heavy-bottomed saucepan and warm the oil. Turn the heat to medium and add the onion, garlic, chilli and herbs. Cook for 5 minutes before adding the mushrooms and corn, seasoning generously with salt and pepper. Turn the heat up a little and cook the mushrooms for 10–15 minutes until golden and their liquid has almost evaporated. Stir in the huitlacoche or truffle oil and potatoes and cook for a further few minutes to allow the flavours to meld. Check the seasoning, cool and stir in the cheese.

THREE CHEESE, HIBISCUS & THYME

A delicious mix of tart, sweet, savoury and cheesy, this filling is very popular with my children and a beautiful colour. Exceedingly good with the Smoky Hibiscus Salsa on page 229, but delicious on its own.

PEA, MINT & FETA

Whenever we have had these on the menu at Wahaca
they have been a total winner. The light sprinkle of chilli gives
the filling a lighter-than-light sparkly dance of flavour and heat
so even my lot will devour them. If you have friends who are
avoiding dairy, leave the feta out of the filling and use it to
sprinkle over the top for those that want that delicious creamy,
salty sprinkle.

1–2 tbsp olive oil

150g (5oz) spring onions (scallions), finely chopped

2 garlic cloves, finely chopped

½ fresh jalapeño, finely chopped (optional)

250g (9oz) peas

100g (3½oz) new potatoes, cooked and diced

15g (½oz) mint

juice of ½ lime

100g (3½oz) feta

salt and pepper

Warm the oil in a pan and add the spring onions, garlic and chilli,
if using. Season generously and sauté gently for 6–8 minutes
until softened. Blanch the peas for a few minutes in boiling
water. Stir into the spring onion with the potato,
mint and lime juice. Check the seasoning
and stir in the feta.

35g (1oz) dried hibiscus flowers

30ml (1fl oz) olive oil, plus a knob of butter

200g (7oz) red onions, finely sliced

1 large garlic clove, crushed

1–2 tbsp thyme leaves

1 tbsp brown sugar

4 tsp sherry vinegar

20g (¾oz) Chipotles en Adobo (page 234)

200g (7oz) crumbled Lancashire, feta or a mix of any young cheeses

salt and pepper

Cover the hibiscus flowers in 400ml
(14fl oz) water and simmer gently
for 25–30 minutes or until tender.

Heat the oil and butter in a sauté pan and
add the onions and garlic. Sweat gently for
10 minutes over a medium heat, then add
the thyme, sugar, vinegar and chipotle.
Season well with salt and pepper.

Drain the flowers, reserving the liquid for
an agua or cocktail (pages 208–23). Finely chop
the flowers and add to the onion with
2 tablespoons of the hibiscus water. Cook for
a final 5 minutes, remove from the heat,
allow to cool, and then stir in the
cheese mix.

TAMALES
WITH SHREDDED COURGETTES & CASCABEL

Nothing takes me back faster to my year in Mexico City than these small dumplings. Street vendors walk through the evening streets calling out, 'Tamales! Tamales! Ricos tamales!'. I can close my eyes now and I am back there, about to head into Prima, the restaurant and bar we opened way back, whose cocktail bar I ran for a few crazy months. The original recipe uses whipped lard but here I make them with coconut oil instead and fill them with feather-light courgettes and a beautifully sweet and nutty tasting salsa.

MAKES 10 TAMALES

100g (3½oz) coconut oil
(or softened butter)

250g (9oz) white or blue corn flour
(not the white cornflour used
as a thickening agent in baking)

2 tsp baking powder

450ml (16fl oz) vegetable stock

½ tsp salt

Sweet Cascabel & Tomatillo Salsa
(page 229) or any other red salsa
you want to use

sour cream or Cashew Nut 'Crema'
(page 242) (optional)

FOR THE COURGETTE FILLING

4 large courgettes (zucchini),
about 1.3kg (3lb)

2–3 tbsp olive oil

2 red onions, finely chopped

3 garlic cloves, finely chopped

1 green chilli, finely chopped (optional)

1 tsp salt

4 thyme sprigs

large handful of coriander (cilantro),
roughly chopped

60g (2oz) hard sheep's or goat's
cheese or Lancashire cheese
or plant-based cheese, plus extra
to serve

You will need parchment pieces roughly 30 x 20cm (12 x 8 inches) or corn husks or banana leaves.

Coarsely grate the courgettes. Heat a large frying pan over a medium heat and, once hot, add the oil, followed by the onions, garlic and chilli. Season with the salt and cook for about 8 minutes until the onion is softening and turning translucent. Add the courgettes, thyme and coriander and cook for a further 10 minutes, stirring every few minutes.

Meanwhile, make the masa – the tamale dough. Using a balloon or electric whisk, whisk the coconut oil deftly until soft, fluffy and pale. Whisk in half the flour and the baking powder, followed by the stock, bit by bit, and finally the rest of the flour. Taste the dough and season with the salt.

If you are using corn husks, you will need to soak them in water to make them supple. If you are using parchment, take 70g (2½oz) of the dough, roll it into a ball and pat it down into the centre of the parchment in an oblong-ish circle, about 5cm (2 inches) long. Add a level tablespoon of courgette mixture to the middle of the dough and a teaspoon of cascabel salsa on top. Finish by crumbling over a little cheese and then, taking them into your hands, fold the masa over the filling. Do not worry too much about completely wrapping it. Wrap the parchment paper around the tamale like a present and steam for 50 minutes or until the masa is just set and firm to the touch.

Serve with extra courgette and salsa on the side and, if you like, a little extra crumbled cheese and sour cream or crema.

GRIDDLED LEEKS
WITH ANCHO & HAZELNUT ROMESCO

Romesco is a rich, smoky sauce from Catalonia, which harnesses the sweet flavours of roast tomatoes and garlic with nuts and chillies. The ancho chilli is similar to the Spanish Nora often used in romesco, so it feels like a natural Mexican accent. A deep, beautiful tasting sauce for these griddled leeks.

SERVES 4 (VO)

6 medium leeks, trimmed

rapeseed (canola) or olive oil, for brushing

1 tbsp chopped tarragon leaves

salt and pepper

FOR THE SAUCE

60g (2oz) hazelnuts, plus 1 tbsp for garnish

2 red peppers, halved and de-seeded

2 large ripe tomatoes, halved

6 unpeeled garlic cloves

2 ancho chillies, stem and seeds removed

140ml (5fl oz) extra-virgin olive oil

1 small slice sourdough or other peasant-style bread

2 tsp sweet smoked pimentón

2 tbsp red wine vinegar

½–1 tsp light brown soft sugar

Preheat the oven to 200°C/180°C fan/400°F/gas 6, put the hazelnuts on a tray and toast for 5–10 minutes until pale golden. Do put a timer on as they burn easily!

Line a large baking tray with parchment paper and lay out the peppers and tomatoes, skin side up. Roast for 10 minutes, then add the garlic and roast for 20–25 minutes until the peppers and tomatoes are blackened all over and the skins are shrivelled. Cover with another baking (cookie) sheet for 10 minutes, then peel the peppers and garlic.

Halve the leeks along their length and rinse. Put in a second baking dish, cut side down, and fill with 1cm (½ inch) of water. Bake for 15 minutes until they have softened. Drain and set aside.

Meanwhile, heat a frying pan (skillet) over a medium heat and toast the ancho chilli pieces for a minute or until fragrant. Tip them into a bowl, cover with boiling water and soak for 10 minutes. Heat 2 tablespoons of the oil in the same pan and gently fry the bread until golden on both sides. Roughly chop the extra hazelnuts for your garnish.

Using a large pestle and mortar or food processor, grind the hazelnuts, peeled garlic, drained chillies, pimentón, bread and ½ teaspoon of salt to a paste. Pummel in the tomatoes and peppers, then work in the vinegar and remaining oil. Taste and season with salt, pepper and brown sugar. If the sauce is very thick, thin with a splash of water.

Heat a griddle pan over a high heat, rub the leeks with oil, season and lay them out in a single layer. Press down with a heavy pan and grill for a 3–4 minutes per side until nicely marked.

Serve the leeks over the romesco, on a warmed plate, scattered with the extra nuts, tarragon and a final flourish of olive oil.

COOK'S NOTE The romesco goes very well with any kind of chargrilled vegetable, especially asparagus.

QUESADILLA

At its simplest, a quesadilla is a flour or corn tortilla filled with local herbs and a fresh string cheese made in Oaxaca, which, like mozzarella, oozes and stretches in the most indecent way when toasted. In Wahaca we mix various cheeses that try to combine some of the melting quality of *quesillo* and a little of its fresh-faced flavour and barely-there acidity. Depending on where you are in Oaxaca, and across Mexico, your quesadilla can be filled with many other ingredients, from epazote and a smear of asiento to sautéed courgette flowers, black beans or huitlacoche, a truffle-like fungus that grows on corn (page 98). You do not need an enormous amount of cheese to make these mouthwatering creations but do experiment with different varieties and flavours. And, with the explosion of increasingly good plant-based cheeses available, even quesadillas can make it onto a plant-based menu. Use up leftovers to fill your quesadillas or stuff them with tried-and-tested favourites cooked from scratch.

Any of the fillings below would also work beautifully astride a tlayuda, a Mexican pizza (page 178).

THREE-CHEESE QUESADILLAS

Oozing, packed with flavour and with that requisite cheesy tang, we have found this is a great balance of cheeses to put inside a plain quesadilla, or one with a simple filling like black beans, fresh herbs or sautéed courgette flowers.

TO FILL ENOUGH QUESADILLAS FOR A LARGE FAMILY/GET TOGETHER

250g (9oz) mozzarella

250g (9oz) mature Cheddar cheese

100g (3½oz) Lancashire cheese or feta

handful of finely chopped parsley, tarragon and chives (optional)

tortillas (page 245)

Fill each 25cm (10 inch) quesadilla with approx. 80–100g (3–3½oz) cheese or smaller tortillas with about 60–80g (2–3oz), depending on how cheesy you want yours. Then try some of the fillings here that I have been making over the years.

BLACK BEANS, FETA & ANISE

Use the cheese mix to the left and add the black beans on page 75, preferably spiked with a little Chipotles en Adobo (page 234).

PICKLED HIBISCUS, SWEET RED ONIONS, CHIPOTLE SALSA (PAGE 228)

The sweet-sour flavours of hibiscus flowers are unbelievably delicious in a quesadilla. Try this one with a mix of Lancashire cheese and Cheddar.

FILLINGS

SAUTÉED MUSHROOMS, CHIPOTLE, FETA

Either go for the garlicky, chilli-spiked mushrooms on page 147 or the truffly ones on page 98 – both will make a brunch or supper fit for a queen.

POBLANO RAJAS (PAGE 14)

Strips of poblano chillies with sweet, sautéed onions and garlic are a great pairing for a more mature cheese like Lincolnshire Poacher.

GARLIC, SOY & LIME CAULIFLOWER, CHIPOTLE MAYO (PAGES 94 AND 240)

Salty, smoky, bold flavours – pure genius.

GRILLED LETTUCE, PEA, MINT & GOAT'S CHEESE

Full of the flavours of summer, I like to grill the lettuce in a griddle pan or over a fire. Try dill, tarragon and parsley as other interesting herbs to throw in. Mix with a fresh young goat's cheese or curd.

NEW POTATOES, CHEESE, THYME

A classic for a reason. Steam new potatoes and toss in sweet, sautéed onions flavoured with jalapeño, lime and thyme. Fold through the Lancashire or feta. If you eat meat, this would be your base for a chorizo quesadilla.

COURGETTE FLOWERS, TARRAGON, SMOKED CHILLI

Sautéed courgette flowers with shallots, garlic, herbs and a touch of chipote.

JERUSALEM ARTICHOKE, TRUFFLE OIL, PECORINO

Steamed, then chargrilled slices of Jerusalem artichoke tossed with black pepper, truffle oil and a roughly grated young vegetarian pecorino make a great substitute for the Mexican delicacy, huitlacoche.

COURGETTES, RED CHILLI, GARLIC & MINT

Flash-fry courgettes (zucchini) with garlic and chilli until golden and lightly caramelised. Toss with fresh lime, chopped mint or tarragon and the three-cheese mix opposite.

WATERCRESS & GRILLED SPRING ONIONS

Watercress and grilled (broiled) spring onions (scallions) are delicious with a mature Cheddar cheese.

GRILLED LEEKS, OREGANO, GOUDA

Sweet sautéed leeks could have been made for a quesadilla. Sprinkle with Mexican oregano and toss with an aged sweet, nutty Gouda cheese.

WILD GARLIC GORDITAS
WITH GRILLED ASPARAGUS & HERBY RICOTTA

Gorditas are little corn cakes. These garlicky, emerald-green ones are made by blitzing wild garlic through the dough and make a brilliant start to a dinner.

MAKES 14–16 GORDITAS

350g (12½oz) masa harina

1½ tsp baking powder

70g (2½oz) wild garlic (ramps) leaves or 90g (3oz) spinach + 1 large clove of garlic, minced

3 tbsp olive oil, plus extra for the asparagus and gorditas

300ml (10½fl oz) boiling water

300g (10oz) asparagus spears

salt and pepper

FOR THE RICOTTA

250g (9oz) ricotta

1 small garlic clove, crushed

4 tbsp good olive oil

30g (1oz) mixed soft herbs, like chervil, mint, dill, tarragon, parsley, chopped

salt and pepper

TO SERVE

Sweet Cascabel Macha (page 229) or your favourite chilli oil

finely grated vegetarian pecorino or Parmesan (optional)

lime wedges

Drain the ricotta in a sieve while you make the gorditas. Combine the masa and the baking powder with a whisk in a large bowl. Wash the wild garlic in cold water and shake dry. Empty into a blender and blitz on full speed with the olive oil and a third of the boiling water until it forms a smooth purée. If you are using spinach, add the washed leaves along with the garlic. Mix in all but a few tablespoons of the rest of the water, then empty over the masa in a large bowl. Use the last of the water to swill around the blender to get every bit of wild garlic purée out. Season generously with salt and pepper and knead with your hands until you have a smooth dough. Set aside for 20 minutes, covered with a damp cloth.

Now mix the garlic, olive oil and herbs into the ricotta and season with salt and pepper.

Preheat a griddle pan or grill (broiler) to its highest setting, toss the asparagus in 2 tablespoons of oil, season and grill for 4–5 minutes, turning to cook evenly. Once cooked, turn off the pan or grill and leave the asparagus there to keep warm.

Roll the dough into small balls and flatten into rounds approx. 5cm (2 inches) wide and 1cm (½ inch) thick with the palm of your hands. Keep covered with the damp cloth. Heat a heavy-bottomed frying pan (skillet). Using a tortilla press and two pieces of parchment paper, flatten the balls out into small rounds about 6–7cm (2½–2¾ inches) across, and no thinner than 3mm (¼ inch) – thicker than a normal corn tortilla. Lightly oil the pan. Cook on each side for a few minutes until toasted.

Top the gorditas with the ricotta, asparagus, and serve with a drizzle of the chilli oil. A sprinkling of finely grated pecorino or Parmesan would not go amiss. Serve while hot with lime wedges.

COOK'S NOTE If wild garlic and asparagus are out of season, use spinach or chard leaves for the dough and grilled broccoli on top.

ALL IN A BOWL

Light, herb-scented broths; warming bowls of silky-soft beans; roasted tomatoes blitzed with softened tortillas; deep bowls full to the brim with all kinds of vegetables. Any country with a love of cooking will show an affinity for soups and broths in its cuisine, but in Mexico it calls your attention loud and clear. Workers' canteens cooking the menu '*del dia*' will invariably have a soup-based starter made from Mexico's seasonal vegetables. More formal and expensive cantinas will boast several soups to start the meal. Street-food stalls sell warming bowls of pozole (delicately scented broths made with stock, herbs, corn and dressed with slaw, fresh lime and salsa). So too the everyday home cook will have several different versions in their repertoire to rustle up these fast-turnaround but endlessly comforting bowls of vegetables at night, when the food is typically light after the famously long and late Mexican lunch.

Soups aside, such is the love affair with Italian cooking that at home many Mexicans will eat pasta for dinner. This is not pasta as we know it, flavoured with basil and balsamic, but pasta dressed with Mexican flavours and ingredients. Dried red chillies gently cooked with many cloves of garlic in oil that stains rusty-red; peppers and milder chillies roasted, peeled and puréed to make thick, creamy sauces; comforting bowls of grains gently flavoured with vegetables and herbs to produce wholesome all-in-a-bowl suppers. This is a chapter both for summery soups and richer, warming autumnal bowls, with relatively quick-to-prepare recipes for those times when something simple and nourishing is needed, but nonetheless packed with layers of flavour. A bowl of soup or stew. Even the words make me smile inside.

SUMMER TOMATO & TORTILLA SOUP

The most classic of Mexican soups, stunning to look at, umami-rich and with the best set of toppings I have ever seen on a soup. This makes a seriously classy starter to an alfresco lunch or late summer dinner or make warming bowls when the weather is cooler using tinned tomatoes instead of fresh. For a different topping, try the Chilli-lime-salt Almonds on page 143 with a swirl of coriander oil. Delish.

SERVES 6 (VO)

2 large onions, peeled and cut into wedges

1kg (2¼lb) ripe tomatoes

4 garlic cloves, unpeeled

2 red chillies

4 tbsp olive oil

1 tbsp chipotle paste

1 tbsp brown sugar

1 tsp dried oregano

1.5 litres (1½ quarts) vegetable stock

2 corn tortillas (page 246), torn into smaller pieces

salt and pepper

TO FINISH

1 large or 2 small avocados, diced

small handful of chopped coriander (cilantro)

zest and juice of 1 lime

2 ancho chillies, stems and seeds removed, torn into small pieces

2 corn tortillas (page 246)

100g (3½oz) feta, crumbled (optional)

Put a large frying pan (skillet) over a high heat and add the onion wedges, tomatoes, garlic and whole chillies. Dry-roast until they are largely blackened and soft to get a rich, smoky flavour. Roast in two batches if they don't fit in a single layer, or on a large, lined tray under a very hot grill (broiler). The garlic and chillies will take 5–8 minutes, the onions and tomatoes 10–15.

Discard the skins of the garlic and the stems of the chillies and transfer to a food processor along with the tomatoes. Whizz until smooth.

Now heat a large casserole dish over a medium–high heat. Once hot, add 3 tablespoons of the oil and the tomato mixture, lower the heat to medium and stir briskly for a few minutes. Season well with salt and pepper and add the chipotle paste, sugar and oregano. Cook for 5 minutes, add the stock and tortillas and simmer for 10 minutes.

Whizz the soup again with a hand blender until smooth, adding a few tablespoons of water if needed to loosen. Taste, adjust the seasoning and simmer gently while you assemble the toppings.

Mix the avocado with half the coriander and the lime zest and juice. Heat the remaining oil in a frying pan and when hot, fry the ancho chilli pieces until puffed up – no longer or they will burn and turn bitter. Toast the tortillas in a pan or over a flame and cut into skinny 2mm strips.

Serve the hot soup with the garnishes in bowls to pass around at the table. If in a heatwave, try the soup gazpacho-style, cooling and thirst-quenching. Hot or cold, both are fantastically good.

PUMPKIN SOUP
WITH PUMPKIN SEED SALSA

Use whatever winter squash you can get hold of to make this velvety, warming soup. Crown Prince, Delica and acorn squashes all have beautifully sweet, almost nutty flavours, but pumpkin or butternut squash also work well. The salsa makes plenty – drizzle over burrata or mozzarella for a lovely autumnal salad with bitter leaves. This soup is also delicious with a dollop of crème fraîche and the Salsa Negra on page 226.

SERVES 4–6 (vo)

5–6 tbsp extra-virgin olive oil

2 red onions, finely chopped

2 celery sticks, finely chopped

3 garlic cloves, finely chopped

2 rosemary sprigs, leaves picked and finely chopped

½ tsp ground allspice

½ tsp ground cinnamon

850g (1¾lb) Crown Prince, Delica or other squash, deseeded and cut into wedges

pinch of chilli (hot pepper) flakes or 1 árbol chilli, crumbled (optional)

bay leaves (optional)

Pumpkin Seed Salsa (page 150)

salt and pepper

Heat the oil in a heavy-bottomed casserole dish and add the onions and celery. Season generously with salt and pepper and sweat over a medium heat for 7–8 minutes until the onions have started softening. Add the garlic, rosemary and spices and cook for another 5 minutes so that the garlic and spices have started filling the kitchen with a wonderful smell.

Add the pumpkin or squash and chilli, if using, and carry on sweating the vegetables for another 5 minutes. Pour over 1.2 litres (1¼ quarts) water or vegetable stock (and a few bay leaves, if you have them) and bring to a simmering point. Simmer the vegetables until they are soft, about 20 minutes, and then whizz to a purée with a hand blender.

Serve in deep bowls sprinkled with the salsa.

ALTERNATIVE

Serve the soup with 100g (3½oz) chopped chestnuts in Ajillo Oil (page 120) or olive oil, cascabel chilli and chopped garlic for a beautifully autumnal finish.

WILD GREENS SPRING SOUP

This soup is in the style of those wonderfully delicate broths I have come to love in Mexico. This vividly green one is inspired by Oaxaca's *sopa de guía*, a clear soup made up of all the green parts of the courgette plant, plus kernels of white corn for heft. My version uses either bought or foraged greens and fresh herbs and I think it is one of the most soothing, life-affirming recipes you can make. Team with a hot salsa and a simple cheese quesadilla and you could be in Oaxaca. If you can't get hold of the corn, try spelt or chickpeas instead, or thicken with a little corn masa, as is often done.

SERVES 4–6 (vo)

150g (5oz) pozole corn kernels (hominy), soaked overnight, or sweetcorn

4–5 tbsp extra-virgin olive oil

300g (10oz) onions, finely chopped

2 celery sticks, cut into long batons and finely chopped

½ head of fennel, finely chopped

4 garlic cloves, sliced

2 courgettes (zucchini), cut into small 1–2cm (½–¾ inch) dice

250g (9oz) hardy greens (spring greens or kale), de-stemmed and shredded

1.5 litres (1½ quarts) vegetable stock or water

150g (5oz) soft greens (spinach, nettle or chard), shredded

tarragon, coriander (cilantro), parsley – a large bunch of each, finely chopped (I also love wild fennel and chervil)

bunch of watercress (optional)

juice of 1 lime

salt and pepper

TO SERVE

quesadillas and hot salsa or crème fraîche, diced avocado and salsa (optional)

Drain the pozole (hominy), cover with cold water and simmer for 40 minutes or until tender, salting the water after 30 minutes.

Meanwhile, put a large casserole dish over a medium–high heat for a few minutes. Pour the oil in, turn down to medium and add the onions, celery and fennel, seasoning generously with salt and pepper. Sweat the vegetables for 10 minutes until sweet and translucent, then add the garlic and cook for another few minutes.

Add the courgettes, followed by the hardy greens and stock. If you have chard, add the stalks at this point too, chopped into 2cm (¾ inch) lengths. Bring the soup to simmering point and cook for 4–5 minutes. At this stage you can stop the cooking as the last stage is quick and the soup should be served as soon as it is ready.

Heat some soup bowls and prepare the quesadillas, if you are having any. Now add the soft greens to the soup and cook for another few minutes. Throw in the herbs, saving some for garnish, and watercress, if you are using. Stir, squeeze in the juice of half the lime and taste – the soup needs quite a bit of seasoning, so add more salt and more lime if needed. Serve at once in hot soup bowls with salsa and quesadillas on the side, or with crème fraîche, avocado and salsa.

FIDEUS

WITH CAPERS, SALSA NEGRA & AVOCADO CREAM

These noodles, with Spanish roots, are cooked in what is known as a 'dry soup'. The resulting dish, a favourite in the impeccable cantinas of Mexico City and Veracruz, is served rather like a risotto course, and is the same consistency. It is a joyous dish, particularly with the rich, smoky hot Salsa Negra, a more intense version of Chipotles en Adobo (page 234). Do give it a go, it is bliss.

SERVES 4 (VO)

4 tbsp olive oil

250g (9oz) angel hair pasta or vermicelli

1 x 400g (14oz) tin of plum or chopped tomatoes

1 onion, roughly chopped

2 garlic cloves, roughly chopped

1½ tsp sweet paprika

½ tsp dried oregano

3 tbsp salted capers, soaked in water

1–2 tsp light brown soft sugar

500ml (17fl oz) hot water

salt

TO SERVE

crème fraîche and slices of avocado or Avocado 'Cream' (page 243)

Salsa Negra (page 226)

handful of coriander (cilantro) leaves, roughly chopped

Heat half the oil in a large, deep frying pan (skillet). Add the pasta and fry until at least half is dark golden, but not burnt. Remove to a kitchen-paper-lined plate and wipe the pan out with a damp, clean dish towel.

Blend the tomatoes, onion and garlic in a food processor until puréed.

Warm the remaining oil in the large frying pan and when hot, add the purée along with the paprika, oregano, drained capers and sugar. Simmer for 10 minutes until the sauce is thick and reduced and the flavours are concentrated. Add the hot water and 1 teaspoon of salt to the purée and bring to the boil. Simmer for 5 minutes and check the seasoning – the sauce needs to season the pasta as well – then set aside.

Meanwhile, make the avocado 'cream', if you are going for the vegan version, and the salsa.

When you are ready to eat, heat the sauce, add the pasta, and cook until the pasta is just tender and the sauce is thick, about 5–7 minutes. Serve in shallow, heated pasta bowls with a spoonful of crème fraîche and the avocado slices or the avocado 'cream, a good drizzle of salsa and lots of fresh coriander sprinkled over.

COOK'S NOTES Fideus is often served with shellfish. If you eat seafood, try cooking clams in the tomato broth or mix brown crab meat into the base of the dish and top with the white crab meat and salsa negra.

ONE-POT BEANS 'N' GREENS

A guisado is a soupy kind of stew and here I make a simple one-pot version using meaty pinto beans, lots of chard, the mild and fruity-tasting guajillo chilli and some Mexican spices. It is a wholesome, comforting bowl of food, great with crispy tortillas (page 247) but also delicious scooped up with tortillas and a roast salsa on the side. And don't panic if you don't have any guajillo chilli, experiment with the equally delicious ancho, cascabel, Aleppo or Korean chilli flakes.

SERVES 4–6 ⓥⓞ

4 tbsp extra-virgin olive oil

1 large leek, washed, halved lengthways and sliced

2 celery sticks, finely chopped

1 carrot, peeled and diced

large bunch of coriander (cilantro), stalks finely chopped

2–4 guajillo chillies

3 large garlic cloves, finely chopped

1½ tsp cumin seeds

6 cloves

1 tsp ground allspice

2 tsp Mexican oregano or fresh oregano or thyme

450g (1lb) Swiss or rainbow chard, stalks sliced into 1cm (½ inch) wide pieces, leaves cut into ribbons

2 x 400g (14oz) tins of pinto beans, rinsed and drained, or 250g (9oz) dried pinto beans, cooked (page 247)

1 x 400g (14oz) tin of chopped tomatoes, drained

salt and pepper

TO SERVE

crispy tortillas (page 247)

sour cream or Cashew Nut 'Crema' (page 242) (optional)

chilli oil, Salsa Negra (page 226) or salsa

Warm the oil in a large casserole dish over a medium–high heat. Add the leek, celery, carrot and coriander stalks, turn down the heat and start to fry gently in the oil.

While they are cooking, de-stem, deseed and roughly chop the chillies. Add to the sautéing vegetables. After 10 minutes, add the garlic, spices, oregano and chard stems, season generously and continue to cook for 4–5 minutes. Add the tinned or cooked beans and pour in the tomatoes, filling the tomato tin twice with water and adding to the pan. Simmer gently for 5 minutes. Now taste and adjust the seasoning with more spices, oregano, salt or a pinch of sugar.

This tastes much better if allowed to sit in the fridge for a day (like all good stews). Serve with crispy tortilla strips, sour cream or crema and a drizzle of chilli oil and your favourite salsa.

COOK'S NOTES If you like cooking beans from scratch, see page 247 for a simple method using any type of bean grown locally to you. In the winter, I love to make this with cavolo nero or kale and the Garlic-fried Chestnuts on page 120.

SWEETCORN POLENTA
WITH CHESTNUTS & GIROLLES 'AL AJILLO'

In the late summer, corn abounds in the markets and small baskets of girolles pop up in delis and greengrocers. Girolles, one of the easiest mushrooms to forage thanks to their distinctive shade of orange-ochre and their posy-like shape, are highly prized for their delicate, peppery flavour, which contrasts beautifully here with the sweetcorn polenta. 'Al ajillo' is a term used to describe anything cooked in an oil flavoured with caramelised garlic and guajillo chillies. It has a sweet, rounded flavour and a barely there heat that is classically paired with shrimp in coastal parts of Mexico, or with mushrooms when they are in season.

SERVES 4

4–6 corn on the cob

½ tbsp salt

180g (6½oz) coarse polenta or corn semolina

40g (1½oz) butter

generous grating of nutmeg

60g (2oz) vegetarian Parmesan, pecorino or hard goat's cheese, grated

FOR THE MUSHROOMS

50g (2oz) butter

2 garlic cloves, chopped

400g (14oz) girolles or other mixed mushrooms

handful of tarragon leaves, finely chopped, plus extra for garnish

100g (3½oz) whole cooked chestnuts, roughly chopped

120ml (4fl oz) Ajillo oil (page 236)

1 cascabel chilli, cut into small pieces with scissors (optional)

juice of ½ lime

Using a large knife, cut the kernels from the cobs and transfer them to a bowl. Put the trimmed cobs and salt into a medium pan with 1.5 litres (1½ quarts) water and bring to the boil. Simmer for 5 minutes to infuse the water, before removing the cobs from the liquid and chucking out.

Whisk the polenta into the simmering water for a few minutes to avoid clumps. Turn the heat right down and cook for 15 minutes, stirring often with a wooden spoon. Add the corn kernels to the pan and cook for a further 10 minutes, adding a dash of water if the mixture becomes too stiff.

Meanwhile, cook the mushrooms. Heat a large frying pan (skillet) over a medium–high heat. Add the butter and when sizzling, add the garlic and mushrooms. Sauté for 10–15 minutes, stirring often, then add the tarragon, the chestnuts, 4 tablespoons of the ajillo oil and the cascabel, if using. Cook for a further 5 minutes until it is all smelling delicious and looking good enough to dive in to.

Once everything is ready, add the butter and nutmeg to the polenta and stir in the grated cheese. Squeeze the lime over the mushrooms and serve the corn in warm bowls, topped with the mushrooms, the remaining ajillo oil drizzled over and a sprinkle of fresh tarragon.

HONEY-ROAST CARROTS
WITH GARLICKY BEAN MASH

The indigenous Mexican diet is full of bean and pulse purées, ladled into, or scooped up with, toasted tortillas. Here I use marrowfat peas, which are a creamy and fun alternative to white beans or chickpeas and one that Hodmedod's is growing across parts of the UK. It makes the most delicious purée for the roast carrots, which are spiked with the mild, fruity guajillo chilli (pages 14 and 17 for more info on chillies). Alternatively, just use chickpeas or butter beans.

SERVES 4

350g (12½oz) dried peas or beans, soaked overnight (page 247 for preparation) or 2 x 400g (14oz) tins of chickpeas, drained and rinsed

20g (¾oz) guajillo chillies, de-stemmed, deseeded and opened up like a book

180ml (6fl oz) olive oil

4 garlic cloves, roughly chopped

1½ tbsp runny honey

750g (1lb 10oz) carrots, peeled and cut into 3–4cm (1¼–1½ inch) rough pieces

juice of ½ lemon

small handful of parsley, roughly chopped

salt and pepper

warm corn or flour tortillas (pages 245–6), to serve

Prepare the peas or beans first. Drain them of their soaking liquid, then cover in enough fresh water to cover by at least 5cm (2 inches). Bring to the boil and simmer for 40 minutes–1 hour until completely tender. Take off the heat and stir in 1 teaspoon of salt. Skip this step if using tinned chickpeas.

Preheat the oven to 220°C/200°C fan/425°F/gas 7.

Put the chillies in a small bowl, cover with boiling water and soak for 10 minutes until soft, then drain and finely chop.

Meanwhile, warm the olive oil and garlic in a medium pan and simmer over a very low heat for 4–5 minutes until fragrant, but the garlic has not coloured. Scoop 60ml (2fl oz) of garlicky oil into a bowl and add the chopped chillies and honey and season generously. Blitz to a purée with a hand blender – do not worry that some of the chilli skin won't purée.

Put the carrots on a baking tray lined with parchment paper and tumble them in the chilli oil. Roast in the oven for 30–35 minutes, stirring once, until the carrots are sticky and a little crisp on the edges.

Meanwhile, blitz the cooked peas or chickpeas with a hand blender with the remaining garlic oil and any water needed to create a nice loose purée, about the consistency of a loose mash. Return to the pan and heat through. Squeeze in the lemon juice and taste, adjusting the seasoning if necessary.

Once the carrots are cooked, serve them on top of the warm pea purée, scattered with the parsley and with warm tortillas for scooping it all up.

CHARRED POBLANO LINGUINE
WITH HOJA SANTA

I know how irritating it is to put obscure ingredients as the focus points of a dish, but this incredibly simple pasta dish is a revelation if you can get past that. Hoja santa is a herb that grows throughout Mexico and is now available dried. The inimitable food writer Diana Kennedy once gave me some to grow and it was the most delicious herb to have in a pot. It is definitely worth seeking out, or replace with a little extra tarragon, dill or even wild fennel (which grows like a weed in any garden). Poblanos grow easily in the UK in the summer, so make this when you can buy them fresh, or buy tinned.

SERVES 4 (VO)

420g (15oz) poblano peppers

1 onion, peeled and cut into wedges

3 garlic cloves, unpeeled

3 tbsp extra-virgin olive oil

50g (2oz) coriander (cilantro) leaves and roots

30–40g (1–1½oz) tarragon leaves (you can discard the tough stalks)

2 tsp dried hoja santa or 50g (2oz) fresh

400g (14oz) linguine

salt and pepper

TO SERVE

good grating of nutmeg

generous sprinkle of grated hard sheep's cheese (optional)

small handful of toasted pine nuts

Cook the peppers, either under a hot grill (broiler) or straight over a gas flame with a pair of tongs, turning regularly until they are charred all over and the flesh is soft, about 10 minutes. Transfer to a bowl, cover tightly and leave to steam.

Meanwhile, heat an old frying pan (skillet) over a high heat and dry-roast the onion and garlic, turning regularly until slightly blackened and charred all over (page 244).

Remove the peppers from the bowl and scrape off the skins, using a damp, clean cloth. Make a slice down one side to open out and remove the seeds. Transfer the poblanos, onions and garlic to a powerful, upright food blender and blitz with the oil, herbs and 80ml (2½fl oz) cold water for at least 2–3 minutes until smooth and aerated. Season generously – it will take quite a bit of salt and pepper.

Bring a large pot of well-salted water to a boil (the Italians say pasta water should taste like the sea). Cook the pasta to al dente, according to the directions on the box. When done, drain the pasta through a colander, reserving a cup of the pasta water. Empty the pasta back into the pan and stir in the poblano cream, pouring in the reserved pasta water bit by bit.

Grate over the nutmeg, add a handful of cheese and serve at the table with more cheese, the toasted nuts and a scattering of herbs. I love this with a green salad or try with the slaw on page 140.

COOK'S NOTES Try swapping in spinach for the chillies - it works like a dream, especially with some double (heavy) cream or with the chilli-lime-salt almonds on page 143 instead of the pine nuts.

HOW TO BUILD

THE CORE

1. Black beans
2. Pinto beans
3. Borlotti beans
4. White beans
5. Lentils
6. Peas
7. Pulses

The core to the engine and an excellent source of both protein and fibre. Preferably served warm!

FRESH AND RAW

1. Massaged kale
2. Slaw
3. Kimchi
4. Rocket
5. Ribboned courgette

Pile in the vitamins, the anti-oxidants, some bitter notes, some crunch. Buy it locally or seasonally if you can. Can you grow it in a window box or pot?

THE FOUNDATIONS

1. Red rice
2. White rice
3. Green rice

Dial up if you are hungry or leave out if you aren't. Can be warm or room temperature but never cold. (Pages 82–83.)

We started putting a 'Mexican bowl' on our menu at Wahaca a few years ago, inspired by the beautifully kaleidoscopic, Asian-influenced taco bowls we had been seeing in cool eateries across LA. They remind me of a great 'molcajete' restaurant near where I lived in Mexico City, where a mass of different grilled and raw ingredients would be piled into a Mexican pestle and plonked on the table for you to stuff inside tortillas. I love the very idea of taco bowls and how they've slunk into people's repertoires, unashamedly adopting ideas here and there from different cuisines. Food travels, it borrows, copies, flatters, imitates and that is how recipes have evolved and spread around the world, stealing an ingredient from here and a cooking method from there. These bowls fit into this book because they take some of the best Mexican ideas, flavours, ingredients and garnishes and build them to create a colourful, balanced and nutritionally dense plate of food that should sustain you for many hours. Add as little or as much as you want of the different elements depending on how hungry you are. It's a pretty sexy way to use up leftovers.

A TACO BOWL

HEARTY AND COOKED

1. Roast sweet potato
2. Roast celeriac
3. Grilled broccoli
4. Grilled asparagus
5. Roast carrots
6. Grilled spring onions
7. Chargrilled aubergine
8. Chargrilled courgette

HUNGER BOOST

1. Feta
2. Lancashire cheese
3. Crumbled goat'S cheese
4. Sliced avocado
5. Sautéed tofu

Add some bulk, some sweetness, great flavour, more fibre. Keep it seasonal to lock in flavour and nutrition.

COLOUR AND ACID

1. Pink pickled onions (page 238)
2. Quick pickled cucumber
3. Finely diced red onion
4. Finely slithered spring onions
5. Wedge of lime
6. Sliced radish
7. Carrot ribbons
8. Pickled chillies

For a boost of mouthwatering sour and an explosion of colour.

JUST ADD HERBS

1. Coriander
2. Mint
3. Chives
4. Dill
5. Tarragon
6. Chervil
7. Basil

For an extra layer of flavour and colour - throw in what feels right and what you have that needs using up.

A NUTTY CRUNCH

1. Maple pumpkin seeds
2. Spicy almonds
3. Soy seed sprinkle
4. Arbol nuts

SALSA OR DRESSING

1. Tomatillo salsa
2. Hibiscus salsa
3. Chilli oil
4. Olive oil & squeeze of lime
5. Fresh tomato salsa

CARAMELISED FENNEL, CASCABEL & HAZELNUT ORECCHIETTE

I love this recipe, with sweet notes from the caramelised fennel and hazelnuts but also from the cascabel, whose gently nutty, rounded flavour adds something rather special here.

SERVES 4 (VO)

- 2 large bulbs of fennel
- 50g (2oz) butter or olive oil
- 3 tbsp extra-virgin olive oil
- 3 garlic cloves, sliced
- 8 cascabel chillies
- 80g (3oz) blanched hazelnuts (filberts)
- 150ml (5fl oz) white wine
- 100ml (3½fl oz) vegetable stock or water
- 300–400g (10–14oz) orecchiette
- small handful of tarragon leaves, finely chopped, plus extra to serve
- salt and pepper
- vegetarian pecorino or vegan cheese, to serve (optional)

COOK'S NOTES Cascabels are mild chillies and widely available online, but if you can't get hold of them, sprinkle in ½ teaspoon Aleppo or Korean chilli flakes or, for a hotter finish, one or two crumbled árbol chillies.

Top and tail the fennel bulbs, keeping any fronds but discarding the tough outer layer (perfect for feeding to rabbits or guinea pigs). Cut the bulbs in half and finely slice, then chop.

Melt the butter and half the oil in a large, heavy-bottomed casserole dish. Add the fennel, season well with salt and pepper and cook over a medium–high heat for about 10 minutes, lowering the heat if the fennel threatens to catch. You want to shrink it into a soft, pale brown mass. After 10 minutes, add the garlic and cook for another 5 minutes.

Meanwhile, remove the stems from the cascabels and tear into pieces. Heat a small frying pan (skillet) over a medium–high heat and toast the chillies for 10–20 seconds on both sides until changing colour and fragrant. Try not to burn them or they will lose their lovely flavour and turn bitter. Scoop into a small bowl and cover with boiling water. Set aside for 10–15 minutes to soften.

Put a large pan of salted water on to boil.

Toast the hazelnuts in the same dry frying pan or in a medium oven until pale golden. Drain the chillies and grind with ½ teaspoon of salt in a pestle and mortar, or small grinder, to a smooth-ish paste. Add the hazelnuts and roughly bash to get a rough mixture of smaller and bigger hazelnut crumbs.

Pour the wine and stock or water into the fennel and simmer for 10 minutes while you cook the pasta. Once the pasta is cooked to al dente, drain, reserving a cup of the pasta water. Pour the pasta into the fennel with the tarragon and half the pasta water and stir for a minute to produce a syrupy sauce. Taste and adjust the seasoning and serve at the table with more tarragon, a wedge of pecorino to liberally grate over and the rest of the olive oil to drizzle over.

RAW & CURED

Beets, green tomatillos, purple tomatillos, small tomatoes, big tomatoes, orange tomatoes, red tomatoes, pineapple, fennel, carrots, white cabbage, red cabbage, radishes (piles of), red onions, pumpkins, courgettes, squash flowers (sacks), watermelons, cauliflowers, mangoes, mushrooms (many different types and sizes), lettuces, radicchios, cucumbers, wild herbs, beans (many, many different beans). I can picture those vegetable aisles in Mexico's food markets as I write this, piles of beautifully arranged fruits and vegetables in their myriad shapes and colours, designed to tempt the shopper in. If the weather of this energetic country is sunny, tropical, often humid, usually hot, then much of the food is light, crunchy, pickled, fresh.

Citrus in the shape of fresh lime, lima, Seville orange and grapefruit are used to sharpen and season salads, ceviches and soups. Vinegars made from apples, guava and pineapple are used to make pickles, relishes and cures. Tostadas and salads, ceviches, tropical fruits and wispy, wafer-thin slaws are seasoned and deliciously dressed to whet the palate, quench the thirst and provide a counterbalance to the more substantial braises and stews that come later. So, delve into this wonderful world of Mexican sour with ceviches made from pineapple and beets; a plate of burrata with a sprightly tomato and tomatillo salad and chargrilled courgettes dressed in a chilli and lime dressing that is an absolute favourite of mine (thank you Leo).

Here you'll find invigorating lunches, mouthwatering starters and a lighter take on snacks and nibbles full of produce shredded, sliced, grated and cut; cured, raw, grilled, dressed up. Gut-friendly, palate-pleasing, crispy, crunchy, sour and sweet.

CUCUMBER & WATERMELON SALAD
WITH CHILLI-LIME-SALT

An incredibly simple salad inspired by the fruit vendors who serve refreshing sticks of mango, cucumber and pineapple on the streets of Mexico, dusted with a spiky, more-ish chilli salt. I sometimes swap the watermelon for the Pakistani honey mangoes when they are in season in June.

MAKES A PLATE · VO

½ watermelon, peeled and sliced

2 cucumbers, cut on the bias

juice of 1 lime, plus lime chunks to serve

2 tbsp extra-virgin olive oil

FOR THE CHILLI-LIME-SALT

10g (¼oz) piquin chillies or Urfa chilli (hot pepper) flakes (page 17)

10g (¼oz) fine sea salt

100g (3½oz) caster (superfine) sugar

zest of 1 lime

Blitz the chillies with the salt in a spice grinder or small food processor, then stir in the sugar and lime zest.

Arrange the watermelon and cucumber on a salad dish. Squeeze over the lime, drizzle with the olive oil and dust with the chilli-lime-salt. Serve at once, with extra lime to squeeze over.

CRISPY, CRUNCHY CAESAR SALAD

The Caesar salad was famously created in Tijuana, Northern Mexico, but variations of it soon spread like wildfire around the world. This plant-based one eschews eggs and anchovies in the dressing for an emulsion of garlic, chickpea water and miso (for that bit of va-va-voom). It is utterly delicious and should make you exceedingly popular with friends. You can buy jars of aquafaba (the chickpea water) but it is expensive; instead open a tin of chickpeas, use the water and keep the chickpeas to make a mash for the Honey-roast Carrots on page 122 or for the Summer Bean Tostadas on page 148.

SERVES 4–6 (VO)

650g (1½lb) new potatoes

½ head of garlic

2 tbsp olive oil

salt and pepper

FOR THE DRESSING

4 tbsp aquafaba (chickpea water)

1 tbsp capers

1½ tsp white miso

100ml (3½fl oz) extra-virgin olive oil

zest and juice of ½ unwaxed lemon

1 tbsp vegan Worcestershire sauce

TO SERVE

1 tbsp olive oil

4–5 (100g/3½oz) corn tortillas (page 246), halved and sliced into skinny 1–2mm straws

2–3 tbsp capers

3 heads of little gem lettuce

Preheat the oven to 200°C/180°C fan/400°F/gas 6.

Put the potatoes in a large pan of salted water, bring to the boil and cook for 15–20 minutes until tender. Drain, then steam dry for 5 minutes. Transfer to a baking tray, then lightly crush the cloves of garlic and drizzle over the oil, season with salt and pepper and give the tray a shake to make sure the potatoes are covered. Cook for 25 minutes, shaking the tray a few times during roasting. The potatoes are ready when they are starting to crisp and turn golden at the edges.

To make the dressing, squeeze out the garlic flesh from the cloves into a food processor, add the aquafaba, capers and miso and blitz together. While the food processor is running slowly, add the olive oil through the feeder tube in a thin, steady stream. Continue to blitz for a further 2 minutes or until the consistency has thickened, then add the lemon zest, juice and Worcestershire sauce. The dressing keeps well in the fridge but will need a light whisk before serving.

Heat the oil in a small frying pan (skillet) over a high heat. Test the oil is hot enough and when it makes a tortilla sizzle, add the strips and fry until crisp and golden. Remove the pieces with a slotted spoon onto a plate lined with kitchen paper. Now fry the capers in the same oil until opened up and crispy.

Serve the salad leaves with the potatoes, capers and a generous drizzle of the Caesar dressing. Sprinkle over the crispy tortillas and serve.

BEETROOT CEVICHE
WITH TARRAGON, BLOOD ORANGE & AVOCADO 'CREMA'

As it becomes increasingly apparent how much we have overfished the oceans and how much care we need to take if we are to eat any fish at all in the future, I have started to look for ways to avoid eating it. 'Ceviche-ing' beautiful vegetables, at the peak of their season has become a favourite in my Mexican feasts. If blood oranges are not in season, use a normal one.

SERVES 6 AS A STARTER OR FEWER AS PART OF A LIGHT MEAL (VG)

4 medium beetroot (beets)

2½ tbsp olive oil

30g (1oz) sunflower seeds

1 avocado

1½ tbsp lime juice

2 tbsp chopped coriander (cilantro) stalks plus small handful of roughly chopped coriander (cilantro) leaves

3 radishes

2 spring onions (scallions), finely chopped

small handful of roughly chopped tarragon leaves

fine sea salt

cress or pea shoots, to garnish (optional)

Tostadas (page 247) (optional)

FOR THE DRESSING

1 Scotch bonnet chilli (or a bird's eye)

1 small garlic clove, unpeeled

¼ tsp cumin seeds

1 tsp caster (superfine) sugar

2 tbsp lime juice

7 tbsp extra-virgin olive oil

juice of ½ orange (blood or otherwise)

salt

Preheat the oven to 200°C/180°C fan/400°F/gas 6.

Rub the beetroot with 1 tablespoon of the olive oil, followed by a little fine sea salt, pop into a baking tin and cover with foil. Roast for 1 hour or until tender when pierced with a knife.

Toast the sunflower seeds in a dry frying pan (skillet) until golden. Remove and set aside.

Meanwhile, to make the dressing, put the chilli and garlic in the dry frying pan over a medium–high heat and toast on both sides until blackened all over, about 5–7 minutes. Toast the cumin seeds for 30 seconds in the same pan. De-seed the chilli, cut into quarters and peel the garlic. Pound a quarter of the chilli to a paste in a pestle with the garlic and several pinches of salt, the cumin and the sugar. Work in the lime juice and finally pour in the olive oil and orange juice and stir to combine.

Blitz the avocado with the lime juice, 1½ tablespoons of water and the remaining oil. Add the coriander stalks and 2–3 large pinches of salt and blitz again to a smooth, thick cream.

When the beetroot is cooked, allow to cool for 5 minutes, then pop on a pair of washing-up gloves and rub away the beetroots' skin. Slice into rounds about 3mm (⅛inch), preferably with a mandolin. Arrange them in overlapping circles on a large serving plate and dress with the dressing while still warm. Slice the radishes to paper-thin discs (use the mandolin if you have it). Scatter over the spring onions, coriander and tarragon leaves and the seeds and dot with the avocado cream. Serve at once with the cress or pea shoots and the tostadas, if making.

CARIBBEAN PINEAPPLE CEVICHE
WITH TOASTED COCONUT

Many years ago, I made a memorable trip to Campeche in search of a local spineless lobster fishing co-operative and some chewing-gum tappers in the nearby rainforest. One lunchtime we ate a fearsomely hot but irresistible ceviche by the beach, which we scooped up with crisp tostadas; warm bowls of tender, soupy black beans added body to the feast and tempered the heat of the fruity, fiery habanero chilli. Here is my veggie version, steeped with the flavours of that Caribbean coastline. It makes a great starter or light lunch with the beans or as part of a summer feast.

SERVES 6 AS A STARTER OR FEWER AS PART OF A LIGHT MEAL (VG)

Pink Pickled Onions (page 238)

300g (10oz) pineapple flesh

1 fennel bulb

60g (2oz) coconut flakes

½ cucumber, halved lengthways, de-seeded and finely sliced

½ bunch of radishes, finely sliced

large handful of mint, roughly chopped

FOR THE DRESSING

70ml (2½fl oz) fresh orange juice

1½ tbsp lime juice

2–3 tsp Scotch bonnet or habanero salsa, to taste

salt and pepper

TO SERVE (OPTIONAL)

Tostadas (page 247)

Cooked Black Beans (page 75)

Make the pink pickled onions: they turn a beautiful neon pink after 30–40 minutes cooling in the fridge. Cut the pineapple in quarters, cut away the cores and thinly slice each quarter to get delicate, slender pieces. Remove any tough outer layers of the fennel, cut in half down through the stalk and slice the bulb very thinly. A mandolin will make this job much quicker. Toast the coconut flakes in a dry frying pan (skillet) over a medium heat until mostly a pale caramel colour.

Whisk together the dressing ingredients, seasoning well with salt and pepper. The amount of heat the dressing has will depend on the heat of your habanero salsa.

If you have some corn tortillas, shallow-fry as per page 247 to make the tostadas, or use pitta breads baked crispy in the oven.

Fan out the pineapple and fennel slices, top with the cucumber and radish, then drizzle with the dressing. Scatter over the mint, pickled onions and coconut, taste to check the seasoning and serve at once with the cooked black beans or tostadas.

COOK'S NOTES There are so many delicious habanero salsas now available, or trade in a Scotch bonnet one for a similar flavour profile. The heat of your dressing will depend on the heat of the sauce you go for, so keep tasting and adjust to your liking.

CHIPOTLE 'KIMCHI' SLAW

I adore this light, refreshing take on a kimchi with its smoky hit of chilli. I use pak or bok choy instead of Chinese leaf because I get it at my local market far more easily than hunting down Chinese leaf and I find the result is lighter and more refreshing. This does not have the proper ferment of a kimchi, but plays on the flavours and is mouthwatering in the taco bowls on page 126, astride a tlayuda (page 178) or even tossed into pasta with sautéed garlic and a crumble of Lancashire cheese. I have halved the chilli and successfully fed it to my children, such is its citrussy, sweet, more-ish quality.

SERVES 6

550g (1¼lb) bok choy or Chinese leaf cabbage, finely sliced

50g (2oz) spring onions (scallions), finely sliced

400g (14oz) carrots, peeled and roughly grated

FOR THE DRESSING

15g (½oz) ginger, peeled and minced

10g (¼oz) garlic, peeled and minced

zest and juice of 1 small lime

1 red chilli, roughly chopped

2 tbsp Chipotles en Adobo (page 234)

100ml (3½fl oz) good-quality sherry vinegar

30g (1oz) light brown soft sugar

1 tsp sea salt

TO SERVE

sesame seeds

30g (1oz) coriander (cilantro) leaves, roughly chopped

Make the dressing first. Put all the ingredients in a blender and blitz to a smooth purée.

Mix together the bok choy, spring onions and carrots in a bowl.

Pour over the dresing and (wearing gloves if you want) scrunch the slaw so the dressing is nicely incorporated. Leave to marinate for at least 30 minutes or overnight.

Just before serving, sprinkle over sesame seeds and coriander.

ACHIOTE-GRILLED HALLOUMI SALAD

Lentils are a popular pulse in Mexico and they make a classic soup with pan-fried, caramelised plantain as a garnish. Thinking about that soup got me dreaming of some onions chef Ollie Dabbous once cooked, which were such an exquisite balance of roast sweetness and light pickle that I am still dreaming of them nearly a decade on. Here, I roast the shallots with Pedro Ximénez balsamic vinegar, which is crazily delicious but a normal balsamic will do a grand job. If you can't get hold of achiote, use 1–2 teaspoons of sumac instead, which is a different kind of tart but along the right lines.

SERVES 4–6

6–8 banana shallots (about 400g/14oz)

extra-virgin olive oil

4 tbsp balsamic sherry vinegar

150g (5oz) green lentils

1 garlic clove

1 tsp Dijon mustard

80g (3oz) watercress

1 small apple

small bunch of mint, roughly chopped

salt and pepper

FOR THE HALLOUMI

1 garlic clove

20g (¾oz) achiote paste

zest of 1 lime, plus 2 tbsp juice

1 packet of halloumi, cut into 1cm (½ inch) slices

salt and pepper

Preheat the oven to 220°C/200°C fan/425°F/gas 7.

De-stem the shallots, peel and cut in half lengthways. Arrange them cut side down in a snug tray, in a single layer. Drizzle over 2 generous tablespoons of olive oil, 2 tablespoons of the balsamic vinegar and 5 tablespoons of water. Season generously with salt and pepper, wrap with foil and bake in the oven for 35–40 minutes until the onions are beautifully caramelised and soft.

Meanwhile, in a pan over a medium heat, cover the lentils with plenty of cold, salted water and add the garlic clove, bashed a few times to break it open. Simmer for 15–20 minutes until just tender.

In a pestle and mortar (or bowl), crush the garlic clove with a few pinches of salt and work in the achiote and lime zest and juice. Season with pepper. Coat the halloumi in the achiote marinade.

Whisk the mustard with the remaining vinegar and 3–4 tablespoons of olive oil. Season lightly. Arrange the watercress on a large platter. Peel and dice the apple. When the lentils are cooked, toss in the dressing while still warm and then toss with the shallots and apples. Check the seasoning.

When you are ready to eat, heat a frying pan (skillet) over a high heat, add a small slick of oil and fry the halloumi slices until they are golden on both sides, a few minutes. Lay the lentil salad over the watercress, top with the halloumi pieces and drizzle over the rest of the marinade. Season with the mint and a flourish of black pepper and serve.

BURRATA
WITH FRESH TOMATILLO SALAD

This is a favourite summer salad and one that I have been making in different guises for many years. Make it when fresh tomatillos are in season, or at a pinch use blanched gooseberries for a similar zingy taste. The sweetness of the dressing and tartness of the fruit are in sprightly contrast to the creamy burrata. I like to throw over a sprinkle of almonds tossed in a pan with the chilli-lime-salt so loved in Mexico (page 132). Raspy, chilli-spiked, sugar-crusted almonds; creamy burrata; sweet, sharp tomatoes; good olive oil; fresh lime. Mamma.

SERVES 4

2 shallots, finely diced

1 tbsp cider vinegar

1 tsp caster (superfine) sugar

1 tsp sea salt

zest and juice of 1 lime

240g (8½oz) fresh tomatillos, washed

250g (9oz) mixed tomatoes, the best that you can find

30–40g (1–1½oz) mixed soft herbs, like tarragon, mint and dill, finely chopped

1 large ball, or a few smaller ones, of burrata or mozzarella

75g (2½oz) crème fraîche

2 tbsp good olive oil

salt and pepper

FOR THE NUTS

50g (2oz) skin-on almonds

1 heaped tsp Chilli-lime-salt (page 132)

Mix the finely diced shallots with the cider vinegar, sugar, salt and lime juice. Leave for 10 minutes to soften while you prepare the tomatillos.

Peel the tomatillos of their husks and wipe with a clean, damp dish towel. Cut the tomatillos into paper-thin slices and the tomatoes into thin slices and various-sized wedges. The tomatillos are tart, so they particularly benefit from being cut into slighter pieces. Mix the lot with the lime zest and the chopped herbs, reserving a small amount to garnish. Once the shallot mixture has been sitting quietly for its time, pour over the tomatoes.

Heat a small frying pan (skillet) and add the almonds. Toast gently until starting to colour lightly. At this point, sprinkle the chilli-lime-salt over and toast for another minute or two until it has formed a light sugar crust over the almonds. Remove from the heat and set aside.

Tear apart the burrata or mozzarella into large bite-size pieces and gently mix in the crème fraîche, half the olive oil and season with salt and pepper. Arrange this in the middle of a pretty serving plate with the fruit around it. Drizzle the lot with the last of the olive oil and scatter over the reserved chopped herbs and the toasted nuts. Eat in the sunshine with a spectacular glass of chilled white wine.

CHARGRILLED COURGETTES

WITH WHIPPED FETA
& BLACKENED CHILLI-LIME DRESSING

Chargrilling courgettes on the griddle or the barbecue brings out their sweetness, while also giving them elusive smoky notes. Using a mixture of yellow and green courgettes makes for a particularly lovely-looking salad. This dressing was devised by Leo, Wahaca's development chef, and it is blissfully light, sharp and zingy all at the same time, perfect for dressing the rich courgette flesh.

SERVES 4–6

70ml (2½fl oz) good olive oil

6 large courgettes (zucchini), green and yellow

few large handfuls of watercress or other peppery leaves

50g (2oz) toasted hazelnuts (filberts) (optional)

FOR THE WHIPPED FETA

200g (7oz) feta, drained

180g (6½oz) Greek yoghurt

2 tbsp tahini

zest and juice of 2 limes

FOR THE DRESSING

2 green chillies

12g (½oz) sea salt

handful mint leaves, plus extra for garnish

Blitz the feta and yoghurt with the tahini, lime zest and 1–2 tablespoons of the olive oil. Set aside.

Dry-roast the green chillies in a dry frying pan (skillet) until blackened in spots all over (page 244), then whizz with 50ml (1¾fl oz) water, the salt, mint leaves, 50ml (1¾fl oz) of the lime juice and 25ml (1fl oz) of the olive oil.

Cut the courgettes lengthways into 2cm (¾ inch) slices and toss in 1–2 tablespoons of oil. Grill (broil) on a griddle or over a barbecue until nicely coloured on each side, turning with tongs. Once they are coloured and tender but not mushy, remove them from the barbecue onto a serving plate.

Spoon the whipped feta onto a pretty platter, followed by the courgettes. Drizzle with some of the lime dressing. Strew with the watercress and then top with toasted hazelnuts, if using, and the mint leaves. Dress with a little more chilli-lime dressing and serve.

A PLATE OF PICKLED VEG

These pickled vegetables appear on cantina tables the length and breadth of Mexico. Their piquant flavour and pleasing crunch make it hard not to polish off a whole bowl in one sitting, which I frequently do when sitting in Contremar, a restaurant that makes a famously good version. Use them to spice up tacos and quesadillas or eat as they come. The chillies give the pickle a tantalising, sparkling heat. Yes, yes!

FILLS A MEDIUM-SIZE KILNER JAR

2 tbsp olive oil

2 large carrots, sliced about 1cm (½ inch) thick on the bias

1 small head of cauliflower, cut into florets

6–8 jalapeño chillies, cut into quarters lengthways, keeping as many of the seeds as possible

8 garlic cloves, peeled and sliced lengthways in half

1 tsp coriander seeds

6 allspice berries, battered with a rolling pin

3 bay leaves

2 tbsp brown sugar

2 tbsp sea salt

250ml (8fl oz) good-quality cider vinegar

You will need a large, clean, sterilised Kilner jar.

Heat the oil in a large casserole dish and add the carrots, cauliflower, chillies and garlic. Sauté over a high heat for a few minutes or until starting to colour, then empty into the Kilner jar.

Put the rest of the ingredients, plus 250ml (8fl oz) water, into the pan, bring to simmering point and simmer for 5 minutes to allow the herbs and spices to flavour the pickle. Check the seasoning, adding more sugar, salt or vinegar to balance the flavours to your taste. Turn off the heat and pour over the vegetables in the Kilner jar.

Allow the vegetables to cool in the pickle. Try not to touch for 3 days as the vegetables mellow in their pickle and become increasingly delicious. They will last for at least a month in the fridge in the sealed jar.

ALTERNATIVE

PICKLED VEGETABLE TOSTADA WITH GUACAMOLE

Spread tostadas (page 247) with frijoles (page 75). Top with the pickles, drained of their pickling liquor, then spoon over guacamole (page 62) and a sprinkling of toasted seeds. A scattering of chopped chervil or fresh coriander (cilantro) finishes it off nicely.

GARLIC MUSHROOM TOSTADAS

WITH GOAT'S CURD & HERBS

We had a version of this tostada on the menus at Wahaca after a company *Masterchef* competition. Kiran, the winner, is Vietnamese and his final dish was an assembly of pickled salads inspired by home. They were astonishingly good and were the inspiration for this tostada, which I had for lunch almost the entire time it was on the menu. Not everyone loves the idea of mushrooms served at room temperature, but I promise you this tostada is the bomb. If you can't get hold of goat's curd, whip some fresh young goat's cheese with a few tablespoons of milk.

SERVES 6

240g (8½oz) soft mild goat's curd

3–4 radishes, finely sliced

30g (1oz) hazelnuts (filberts), toasted and roughly chopped

handful of roughly chopped parsley or tarragon, or both

FOR THE MUSHROOMS

600g (1¼lb) mixed mushrooms (such as chestnut, portobello, shiitake, oyster)

5 tbsp rapeseed (canola) oil

3 garlic cloves, sliced

small knob of ginger, peeled and grated

2 guajillo chillies, toasted, rehydrated and finely chopped (page 17)

2 tsp sea salt

3 tbsp red wine vinegar

2 tbsp soy sauce

FOR THE TORTILLAS

vegetable oil, for frying

12 small corn or flour tortillas (pages 245–6) or pitta breads, cut into rounds

Slice the mushrooms into a variety of bite-size shapes – none of them should be too big or they will be difficult to balance on the tostada, but bear in mind that they will shrink when cooked.

Heat your largest sauté pan over a medium–high heat and cook the mushrooms in two batches if they don't comfortably fit in. Pour in a third of the oil. Add half the mushrooms, the garlic, ginger, chopped chillies and sea salt. Stir constantly until the mushrooms start to soften and catch. The time will depend on the size of pan. Once the mushrooms are starting to brown, add a tablespoon each of the vinegar and soy sauce and a tablespoon of oil. Scoop out and repeat with the second lot.

Once they are cooked, return the first lot to the pan and continue to cook all the mushrooms over a medium heat for 10–15 minutes, then turn off the heat and stir in the last of the vinegar. Allow to cool to room temperature.

Warm a couple of centimetres of oil in a small frying pan (skillet) and individually fry the tortillas for approx. 30 seconds on each side until golden and crisp, then drain on kitchen paper. Repeat until you've fried them all and keep warm.

Spread the goat's curd over the tostadas. Top with mushrooms, then radish slices, nuts and herbs and let people tuck in.

COOK'S NOTES If you want to avoid frying, brush the pittas with a little oil and bake in the oven.

SUMMER BEAN TOSTADAS

We have almost always had some form of bean tostada on our menus since we first opened our doors at Wahaca. There is something incredibly good about the mix of soft beans and pulses, crunchy sweet onion, fresh herbs, crispy corn tostadas and some sort of zippy chilli dressing. They are resoundingly healthy as is, but try topping with a blob of the charred Jalapeño Aioli (page 240) for a hard-to-beat extra lick of flavour.

MAKES 4   (vo)

½ small red onion

juice of 1 lime, plus extra wedges, to serve

1 x 400g (14oz) tin of borlotti beans, drained and rinsed

1 x 400g (14oz) tin of chickpeas, drained and rinsed

150g (5oz) ripe tomatoes, roughly chopped

handful each of mint, chervil and parsley, roughly chopped

100g (3½oz) radishes, quartered

5 tbsp habanero dressing, plus extra to serve

salt

FOR THE TORTILLAS

vegetable oil, for frying

12 small corn tortillas (page 246) or pitta breads, cut into rounds

TO SERVE

vegetable oil, for frying

2 baby gem lettuces, shredded, to serve

Twice-cooked Beans (page 75), to serve

Jalapeño Aioli (page 240) (optional)

Place the onion and lime juice and a pinch of salt in a mixing bowl and allow to sit together for a bit to take the edge off the onion while you prepare everything else.

Throw the remaining ingredients into the mixing bowl and toss well to combine. Put to one side to give the flavours some time to mingle.

Warm a couple of centimetres of oil in a small frying pan (skillet) and individually fry the tortillas for approx. 30 seconds on each side until golden and crisp, then drain on kitchen paper. Repeat until you've fried them all and keep warm.

Serve the bean salad, shredded lettuce and warm tostadas together for people to make their own, with the twice-cooked beans and some extra habanero dressing on the side, plus some jalapeño aioli, if you like.

IMAGE OPPOSITE A trio of tostadas: Garlic Mushroom (page 147), Pickled Veg (page 146) and Summer Bean.

MAPLE-PICKLED PUMPKIN & PINK LEAF SALAD

WITH PUMPKIN SEED SALSA

This salad is a kaleidoscopic celebration of both Mexican ingredients and the northern hemisphere's autumn produce, with the vivid-orange pumpkin flesh, neon-pink leaves and the jewel-like seeds of the pomegranate, all set off by the green salsa and white crumbs of the feta. It is a veritable feast.

SERVES 4–6 (VO)

- 300g (10oz) peeled Delica, Crown Prince or butternut squash
- 2½ tbsp sherry vinegar
- 3 tbsp maple syrup
- 70g (2½oz) pumpkin seeds
- 1 tsp sweet smoked paprika
- 2 tsp olive oil
- 2 heads of Treviso or red chicory
- small handful of coriander (cilantro) leaves
- seeds of ½ pomegranate
- 70g (2½oz) feta, crumbled (optional)
- salt and pepper

FOR THE PUMPKIN SEED SALSA

- 50g (2oz) parsley
- 30g (1oz) tarragon
- 1 large garlic clove
- 1 red chilli, roughly chopped
- juice of 1 lemon
- 150ml (5fl oz) olive oil

With the help of a mandolin or a speed peeler, slice the pumpkin into fine, long, slender pieces, as thin as you can. Toss in the sherry vinegar and 2½ tablespoons of the maple syrup, seasoning well with salt and pepper. Cover and refrigerate while you prepare the rest of the salad.

Toss the pumpkin seeds in the rest of the maple syrup, the sweet smoked paprika and olive oil. Toast in a frying pan (skillet) until the pumpkin seeds have popped and are toasted.

Blitz half these seeds with the herbs, garlic, chilli, lemon juice and olive oil to make the pumpkin seed salsa. Season with black pepper and ½ teaspoon of salt and then taste to adjust the seasoning.

Break open the salad leaves, wash, dry and break up or chop into large bite-size pieces. Lay out on a serving plate. Scoop the squash from its pickling liquor and arrange over the leaves, drizzling over half the pickling juice and a third of the pumpkin seed salsa.

Scatter over the coriander, pomegranate seeds, feta (if using) and remaining pumpkin seeds. Season well. Drizzle with a last flourish of the salsa and serve with grilled toast and olive oil for a starter or lunch or as one part of a feast.

TOMATO, PINEAPPLE & FETA FATTOUSH

WITH CRISPY CHICKPEAS

This salad was inspired by a plate of tomatoes and pineapple that was once prepared for me by the wonderful Oaxacan chef Alejandro Ruiz. It was a simple affair, with slices of ripe, juicy tomatoes and those beautifully sweet, acidic Mexican pineapples, which are in a league of their own. It opened my eyes to the versatility of pineapples, which, like tomatoes, are delicious in both sweet and savoury dishes, whether raw, grilled, roasted or stewed into wonderful ketchups and salsas. If you don't have hibiscus flowers, which add a lovely tangy seasoning, use sumac instead.

SERVES 4–6

1 x 400g (14oz) tin of chickpeas, drained and rinsed

3–4 tbsp olive oil

1 tsp hot smoked paprika

1 tsp sweet smoked paprika

1 tsp ground cumin

3–4 corn or flour tortillas (about 50g/2oz cooked weight) (pages 245–6)

12 ripe baby tomatoes, quartered

¼–⅓ pineapple, flesh diced

1 cucumber

10 radishes

small handful of tarragon leaves, roughly chopped

few pinches of dried oregano

juice of 1 lime

50g (2oz) feta

½ tbsp dried hibiscus flowers, ground to a powder, or sumac

salt and pepper

Preheat the oven to 220°C/200°C fan/425°F/gas 7.

Rub the chickpeas dry with kitchen paper, then pour out on to a baking sheet, season well and toss in 1 tablespoon of the oil, the paprikas and the cumin. Roast in the oven for 15–20 minutes until golden and crisp, giving the tray an occasional shake.

Put the tortillas on another tray, brush on both sides with 1–2 teaspoons of oil and bake in the oven until golden (6–8 minutes for corn tortillas or 5–6 minutes for flour). They will crisp more as they cool. Allow to cool before breaking into rough shards and emptying into a mixing bowl with the chickpeas.

Chop the tomatoes, pineapple, cucumber and radishes into pieces the size of the chickpeas, then add to the bowl along with the remaining tablespoon of olive oil, herbs and lime juice. Season, then mix everything together with your hands. Crumble over the feta, sprinkle with a little of the ground hibiscus, then serve.

FAMILY STYLE

The map of my life is shaped around tables: tables full of people, tables laden with food. Every table, every feast, every memory is coloured by the ingredients we ate and the conversations we had. There exists a kind of subconscious scrapbook of joy and life force that resonates and grows through conversation and food, eating and life. In Mexico, this world is exceptionally vivid and even highlighted in its festivals. The Day of the Dead festival is a celebration of lost loved ones and plays up the power of feasting to tempt them back to earth, to sit once more at the table with friends and family and break bread, sip tequila or mezcal and dance.

The recipes in this chapter are a nod to the communal table. They are designed to be filling, nourishing and life-affirming. Recipes that will comfortably be the main meal of the day, a family lunch or supper, or that can become a main course to a larger dinner.

While an enchilada, the Mexican equivalent of an Italian lasagne, usually plays a homely, comforting role, I would feel more than happy to provide the summery aubergine and fresh tomato enchilada, or the smooth celeriac and Swiss chard one with its citrussy tomatillo sauce at a dinner. Try putting down the giant conchiglioni pasta bake, with its roast garlic, sweet ancho and charred tomato sauce on an autumnal lunch table. Stuff a pepper with my raw summery filling, or a more warming, wintery one, and find that it can do relaxed or smart with ease. As for the Mexican pizzas (called tlayudas in Oaxaca), make them one weekend and marvel at how they puff up and blister on a barbecue or grill: you can have wild fun with their toppings and they make the most amazing party food, especially with a great chilli oil (page 236) to liberally drizzle over.

ROAST BEETS
WITH WHITE MOLE

One of my favourite restaurants in the world is in Mexico City, called Rosetta. It is full of light and greenery, beautiful wallpaper and stone fireplaces, high ceilings, large windows and vintage china to show off its stunning food. The incredibly talented owner and chef is Elena Reygadas, who spent several years in London training under the watchful eye of Giorgio Locatelli, among other places. She takes the Italian ethos of simplicity and applies it to beautiful seasonal Mexican ingredients. This white mole is inspired by one I had there. Paired with the roast beetroots, it makes a delicate dish that is arrestingly pretty and wonderfully simple to make.

SERVES 4–6   (vo)

1 white onion, peeled and cut into 8 wedges

4 garlic cloves, unpeeled

90g (3oz) pine nuts

100g (3½oz) blanched almonds

½ tsp ground allspice

½ tsp ground cinnamon

1 tsp sea salt

2½ tbsp cider vinegar

1 tbsp oil

salt and pepper

FOR THE BEETS

800g (1¾lb) beetroot (beets), scrubbed and cut into 3cm (1¼ inch) wedges

4 garlic cloves, unpeeled

3 tbsp olive oil, plus extra to drizzle

3 rosemary sprigs

handful of mint leaves

seeds from ½ pomegranate

salt and pepper

Preheat the oven to 220°C/200°C fan/425°F/gas 7. Line a baking tray with foil.

Toss the beets, garlic, oil and some seasoning together in a bowl, then spread out on the tray and scatter over the rosemary. Roast for 35–45 minutes, by which time the beets should be tender, a little gnarly and crisp at the edges.

Meanwhile, toast the onion and whole garlic cloves in a dry frying pan (skillet), shaking and turning them frequently for 8–10 minutes until charred all over and tender in the middle. When cool enough to touch, peel the garlic.

Put the nuts in a blender or food processor, blitz until fine, then add 100ml (3½fl oz) cold water in a steady stream, blitzing until smooth. Add the charred onion and garlic, the spices, sea salt and pepper, to taste, and blitz again for 40 seconds at least. Add the vinegar and 150ml (5fl oz) water in a slow stream and continue to blitz until smooth.

Now, heat the oil in a small pan and pour in the mole. Cook through for 10 minutes to allow the flavours to get to know one another, adding more water if needed. You want to be able to spoon the mole across a plate. Adjust the seasoning to taste.

When you're ready to eat, spread the warm mole in the middle of warmed plates. Top with the roast beetroot and scatter over the mint and pomegranate seeds. Drizzle with a little extra oil before serving with crusty bread, flatbreads or corn tortillas.

GRILLED HISPI
WITH CELERIAC MASH & ANCHO RELISH

There is something silky about celeriac, which lends itself very well to olive oil, so this dairy-free mash tastes just as spoiling and indulgent as a classic creamy one. The high acidity of the ancho relish adds a delicious piquancy that cuts through it and the chargrilled cabbage, making it a wonderful vivid-tasting dish in the autumn. As with so many things, using a good-quality, mellow vinegar will make the relish especially good. If you don't have time to let the relish sit, consider making this with the Ajillo Oil on page 236 for a slightly different finish and try this recipe with grilled purple sprouting broccoli when the hispi season is over.

SERVES 4 (vo)

2 hispi cabbages, outer leaves discarded, cut into quarters through the stem

big handful of roughly chopped parsley

FOR THE ANCHO RELISH

4 ancho chillies

2 banana shallots, finely chopped

2 fat garlic cloves, finely chopped

75ml (2½fl oz) red wine vinegar

150ml (5fl oz) good olive oil

salt and pepper

FOR THE CELERIAC MASH

60ml (2fl oz) olive oil

1kg (2¼lb) celeriac (celery root), peeled and cut into 2cm (¾ inch) cubes

3 tsp thyme leaves

2 garlic cloves, finely chopped

salt and pepper

First, make the relish. Tear open the chillies, de-stalk and de-seed, then pulse in a food processor to pieces the size of small snowflakes. Transfer to a lidded Kilner jar and stir in the rest of the relish ingredients. Season to taste and leave to macerate. The flavours will keep on improving for several weeks, so make double if you feel up for it or let it sit overnight to allow the garlic and shallots to soften in tone.

For the mash, heat the oil in a large pan over a medium–high heat and add the celeriac. Once it begins to colour slightly, 4–5 minutes, throw in the thyme leaves, garlic and plenty of seasoning. Fry for another 3 minutes or so until the garlic is fragrant, then add 75ml (2½fl oz) water, turn the heat down to a simmer and place a lid on top. Cook for 20–25 minutes, stirring occasionally, until the celeriac is soft. Add splashes of water if it is beginning to stick.

Meanwhile, bring a large pan of salted water to the boil, blanch the cabbage wedges for 3 minutes, then lift out and leave to steam dry. Heat a large griddle pan or grill (broiler) and, once hot, char the cabbage wedges on both sides, until they are covered in dark char marks and the edges are crisp.

Divide the celeriac mash between four warm plates and top each serving with two cabbage wedges. Spoon over some of the relish, then dribble a little oil from the relish over the top. Sprinkle with the parsley and serve at once.

CLASSIC ENCHILADA
WITH SWEET POTATO, SPINACH & BLACK BEANS

A classic Mexican enchilada is either made with a red sauce or a green sauce. When the sauce is red it is made with tomatoes, spices and guajillo chillies for their colour and mild, sweet flavour. Enchiladas take me right back to Mexico City where I lived for a year. This would be what I ate in people's homes and for the *comida corridas*, those brilliantly subsidised, hearty three-course lunches served in city restaurants for next to nothing that could sustain you throughout the day. Serve with green or white rice (pages 82–3) and/or a crisp green salad.

SERVES 4–6

FOR THE SAUCE

3 guajillo chillies

1 red onion, roughly diced

2 garlic cloves, roughly diced

1–2 tsp Chipotles en Adobo (page 234)

pinch of Mexican oregano

½ tsp ground cumin

½ tsp allspice

½ tsp ground cinnamon

1–2 tsp brown sugar

1 x 400g (14oz) tin of plum tomatoes

1½ tbsp olive oil, plus extra for layering

FOR THE ENCHILADAS

1 onion, finely chopped

2 garlic cloves, finely chopped

½ tsp salt

2 sweet potatoes (or any other root veg mix), peeled and diced

200g (7oz) spinach

1 x 400g (14oz) tin of pinto or black beans, drained and rinsed

10 small corn tortillas (page 246)

100g (3½oz) grated cheese

Preheat the oven to 180°C/160°C fan/350°F/gas 4.

De-stem and de-seed the guajillos and toast in a dry hot pan on both sides for 20–40 seconds until they darken and smell fragrant, then cover with boiling water and simmer for 10 minutes to soften while you prepare the rest of the ingredients.

Drain the chillies and put into a blender with the rest of sauce ingredients except the oil and blitz until smooth. Heat half the oil in a casserole dish over a medium–high heat and add the sauce. Stir for a few minutes, then pour in enough water to produce a sauce the consistency of thick cream.

Warm the rest of the oil in a large pan and fry the onion and garlic with the salt over a low heat for 10 minutes until soft and sweet. Add the diced sweet potato and spinach, sweat for 5 minutes, then add a cup of water and cover and steam for 10 minutes until soft.

Pour in half the enchilada sauce and the beans and cook for 5 minutes. Pour half of this into a gratin dish, cover with half the tortillas, drizzle with a little oil and repeat, layering up the sauce and filling. Finish with sauce and scatter with the grated cheese. Or you could make the classic cannelloni-style ones too, by rolling the filling inside the tortillas, then saucing.

Bake for 15–20 minutes until golden and serve at the table.

TOMATO, MOZZARELLA & AUBERGINE ENCHILADA

A rich enchilada using summer tomatoes and aubergines and inspired by the deeply more-ish Sicilian *parmigiana alla melanzane*. The chilli adds a light heat, but leave it out or remove the seeds for a milder taste. If you are feeling the Mexican vibe, serve with thinned-out sour cream, avocado and coriander leaves.

SERVES 4

FOR THE SAUCE

700g (1½lb) ripe tomatoes

1 large red onion, peeled and cut into 8 wedges

4 garlic cloves, unpeeled

1 habanero or jalapeño chilli, de-stalked (optional)

1–2 tsp brown sugar (depending on ripeness of the tomatoes)

1 tsp dried oregano

1 tsp salt

4 tbsp good olive oil

small bunch of tarragon, leaves picked

FOR THE ENCHILADAS

2 large (600–700g/1¼–1½lb) aubergines (eggplants)

3 tbsp olive oil

150g (5oz) grated cooking mozzarella

100g (3½oz) mature Cheddar cheese, grated

80g (3oz) feta, crumbled

big handful of parsley leaves, chopped

2 garlic cloves, finely chopped

12 corn tortillas (page 246)

salt and pepper

Dry-roast the tomatoes, onion, whole garlic cloves and chilli, if using, in a dry frying pan (skillet), shaking and turning them frequently until charred all over. The garlic and chilli will be cooked first, 6–7 minutes, then the tomatoes and onions, 12–14 minutes. Peel the garlic when cool. Empty the lot into a blender with the sugar and oregano. Season with salt and pepper, and blitz until smooth.

Heat the oil in a saucepan over a medium heat and pour in the tomato sauce. Cook, stirring occasionally, for 10–15 minutes until it is rich and has reduced. Stir in half the tarragon, check the seasoning and remove from heat.

Meanwhile, preheat the grill (broiler) to high and cut the aubergines lengthways into roughly 5mm (¼ inch) slices. Brush both sides with oil, season generously and lay out on one or two large baking trays lined with parchment paper. Grill for 3–4 minutes a side until golden and soft.

Preheat the oven to 180°C/160°C fan/350°F/gas 4. Combine the cheeses and set aside 80g (3oz). Toss the rest with the herbs and garlic.

Spoon a third of the tomato sauce into a large ovenproof gratin dish. Briefly warm each tortilla in a pan splashed with a little water to make them supple. Lay a piece of aubergine horizontally across the middle of a tortilla. Dollop 2 tablespoons of the cheese mix in the centre of each aubergine slice, then roll the tortilla over to make a parcel. Repeat, laying each parcel sealed-side down in the sauce, packing them in snugly. Spoon over the remaining sauce and sprinkle with the reserved cheese. Bake, covered with foil, for 25 minutes, then remove the foil and bake for another 10 minutes until the cheese is melted and golden.

CELERIAC & CHARD ENCHILADA
WITH GREEN CASHEW TOMATILLO SALSA

I love anything steeped in a citrussy, fresh tomatillo sauce. There is something deeply mouthwatering about this combination of the tangy sauce and the earthy flavour of corn. This recipe is adapted to be dairy-free, but for a classic version, leave out the cashews and bake with a sprinkle of Lancashire, feta or an aged sheep's cheese and serve with Crema (page 242) or crème fraîche.

SERVES 4 (VO)

5 tbsp olive oil

600g (1¼lb) celeriac (celery root), peeled and cut into 2cm (¾ inch) cubes

2 tsp thyme leaves

2 garlic cloves, finely chopped

bunch of spring onions (scallions), finely sliced

400g (14oz) Swiss chard, leaves separated from the stalks, washed

12 corn tortillas (page 246)

salt and pepper

FOR THE TOMATILLO SAUCE

30g (1oz) raw cashews, soaked in 75ml (2½fl oz) water for 1 hour or overnight

30g (1oz) jalapeño chillies, de-stemmed and de-seeded

large handful of coriander (cilantro) leaves

2 garlic cloves, roughly chopped

10g (¼oz) ginger, peeled and roughly chopped

4 spring onions (scallions), roughly chopped

1 tbsp caster (superfine) sugar

1 tsp sea salt

350g (12½oz) tinned tomatillos, drained weight

Warm a large pan over a medium–high heat, then add half the oil and the celeriac. Once the celeriac is starting to colour, 4–5 minutes, add the thyme, garlic and spring onions and season generously. Fry for another few minutes until the garlic is fragrant, then add 100ml (3½fl oz) water. Bring to simmering point, turn down the heat, cover and cook for 10 minutes.

Meanwhile, slice the chard stalks into 5mm (¼ inch) strips and the leaves into ribbons. Add the chard stalks to the celeriac after the 10 minutes of cooking and cover the pan. Once the stalks are tender, stir in the leaves, adding a little more water if it looks dry. Cover and cook for 7–9 minutes until the chard has wilted and the celeriac is soft. Check the seasoning, then remove from the heat.

Preheat the oven to 220°C/200°C fan/425°F/gas 7.

Empty the cashews and their soaking liquid into a blender and blitz. Add the rest of the sauce ingredients and blitz until smooth, then check the seasoning.

Warm the rest of the oil in a medium pan over medium heat and pour in the sauce. Fry, stirring, for 4–5 minutes until it darkens slightly and the garlic and ginger are fragrant. Spoon a third of it into an ovenproof dish. Now assemble the enchilada either warming and wrapping the tortillas as in Mexico (page 160), or simply layering up, lasagne-style (page 159). Spoon over the rest of the sauce, cover with foil and bake for 20 minutes. Remove the foil and return to the oven for a final 5–10 minutes until lightly coloured. Serve immediately with a green salad if you like.

SMOKY ROAST SQUASH

WITH GREEN CASHEW NUT MOLE

Mole [moll-ay] is the Nahuatl word for sauce – hence guacamole meaning avocado sauce. This blissfully simple dish can really show off the flavours of different squash plants. This simple green herb mole is incredibly versatile and was devised by Carlos Macías, a wonderful development chef.

SERVES 4–6 (VG)

1kg (2¼lb) squash, such as butternut, kabocha or Crown Prince, de-seeded and cut into moon-shaped wedges

1½ tsp sweet smoked paprika

3 tbsp olive oil

Fresh Tomato Pico (page 226)

25g (1oz) pumpkin seeds

50g (2oz) feta (optional)

Ajillo or chilli oil (page 236) (optional)

salt and pepper

FOR THE CASHEW NUT MOLE

150g (5oz) raw cashews

1 tbsp lime juice

2 tbsp cider vinegar

1 green chilli, de-seeded (optional)

big handful each of mint and parsley leaves

½ tsp salt

Soak the cashews in 180ml (6fl oz) water for at least 1 hour to ensure a beautifully smooth, enviably silky mole.

Preheat the oven to 220°C/200°C fan/425°F/gas 7 and line a large baking tray with greaseproof paper. Lay out the squash on the baking tray, rub with the paprika and oil and season generously. Roast in the oven for about 40 minutes until tender and crisp on the edges.

Next, make the tomato pico and put to one side.

Once the cashews have soaked for their hour, put them in a blender with their soaking liquid, lime juice, vinegar, chilli, herbs and the salt. Blitz until you have a bright, lovely smooth purée. Taste and adjust the seasoning with salt and vinegar. Transfer to a pan and warm gently – if you overheat this sauce it will lose its arresting emerald-green colour.

Toast the pumpkin seeds in a small, dry frying pan (skillet) over a medium heat until they begin to darken and pop, about 3–4 minutes. When the squash is done, transfer the warm mole to a large shallow bowl, platter or individual plates. Top with the squash wedges, then spoon over the salsa, scatter with the pumpkin seeds and a little crumbled feta, if you wish. Season lightly, drizzle with chilli oil, if using, and serve at once.

SUMMER POBLANO PEPPERS
WITH CRUNCHY CAULIFLOWER SALAD
& WILD HERB MOLE

Poblano peppers have a mild and grassy flavour (page 14). They are grown in the UK but the season is short. If you can't get hold of fresh, try tinned poblanos or fresh sweet Romanos. This is an impressive-looking dish to give to friends and yet is simple to make. The herb-flecked, crunchy salad provides lovely bursts of flavour against the mellow, creamy mole.

SERVES 4 (vo)

75g (2½oz) red quinoa, rinsed

4 large poblano peppers (or sweet Romano red)

65g (2oz) flaked (slivered) almonds

25g (1oz) sesame seeds

½ red onion, finely chopped

50g (2oz) currants or raisins

2 tbsp good cider vinegar

1 medium head of cauliflower, leaves and core discarded

½ bunch of coriander (cilantro), leaves roughly chopped, stalks finely chopped

½ bunch of parsley, finely chopped

1 carrot, peeled and coarsely grated

juice of 2 limes

4–5 tbsp good olive oil

salt and pepper

TO SERVE

Green Cashew Nut Mole (page 156)

finely chopped red onion

chopped fresh herbs

For the mole, follow the recipe on page 156, soaking the cashews for 1 hour, adding a few handfuls of coriander (cilantro) and a large handful of tarragon leaves.

Put the quinoa in a small pan, cover with water and season with salt. Bring to the boil, then simmer for 15–20 minutes until the grains have unfurled but have a bite. Drain through a sieve and steam dry.

Cook the peppers under a hot grill (broiler) or over a gas flame using tongs, turning regularly until charred all over and the flesh is soft, about 10 minutes. Transfer to a bowl, cover tightly and leave to steam. Meanwhile, place a dry pan over a medium heat and toast the almonds until pale golden all over. Repeat with the sesame seeds, reserving a bit of both.

Cover the red onion and currants with the vinegar and set aside. Using a mandolin or sharp knife, shave the cauliflower into thin slivers. Empty into a mixing bowl and toss with the quinoa, almonds and sesame seeds, herbs, onion, currants, carrot, lime juice and oil. Taste and adjust the seasoning.

Scrape off the skins of the peppers, using a damp, clean cloth. Slice down one side to open out and remove the seeds, then fill with salad.

Spoon the warm mole onto warm plates and top with the peppers. Scatter with the reserved almonds, sesame seeds, red onion, a final flourish of green herbs and serve at once.

ALTERNATIVE

AUTUMNAL SQUASH-FILLED PEPPERS

For a warming dish, fill the peppers with Green Rice (page 83), garlic-roasted squash, sautéed red onions, green olives, fresh herbs and Ajillo Oil (page 236).

BAKED POLENTA
WITH VERACRUZAN SAUCE & SAUTÉED GREENS

This bewitching, silkily rich tomato sauce comes from Veracruz, where Cortés first landed to discover the Americas. At that time the Spanish were also occupying Sicily, so traders brought capers and olives to Mexico and returned laden with cacao, tomatoes and gold. A classic Veracruzan sauce is thus spiked with olives and capers. You can use pickled jalapeños here, but I find pickled Spanish guindillas or pickled Turkish chillies also have great spice and character.

SERVES 6 WITH LEFTOVERS

250g (9oz) coarse polenta

1.2 litres (1¼ quarts) water or vegetable stock

3 tbsp olive oil, plus extra for drizzling

small handful of chopped parsley

vegetarian Parmesan or pecorino or vegan cheese, finely grated (optional)

3 large handfuls of greens (chard, spinach, kale), de-stemmed

salt and pepper

FOR THE SAUCE

3 tbsp olive oil

1 large Spanish onion, finely sliced

2 carrots, diced

2 celery sticks, diced

½ head of garlic, cloves peeled and sliced

handful of oregano leaves or thyme

2–3 bay leaves

100ml (3½fl oz) manzanilla sherry

80g (3oz) good-quality green olives, pitted and roughly chopped

40g (1½oz) capers, roughly chopped

60g (2oz) pickled chillies, sliced, plus extra to serve

1 cinnamon stick

1 tbsp brown sugar

1.2kg (2lb 10oz) ripe red tomatoes or 3 x 400g (14oz) tins of plum tomatoes

Line a 20 x 30cm (8 x 12 inch) baking tin or dish with cling film (plastic wrap) and set aside. Put the polenta in a pan with the water or stock and season well. Cook according to the packet instructions, adding more liquid if needed so it can be poured into the tin. Once cooked, immediately stir in 1 tablespoon of the olive oil, the parsley, lots of salt and pepper, to taste. Pour into the lined dish, smooth the surface and set aside to cool. You can do this up to 2 days ahead – just cover and store in the fridge.

Meanwhile, to make the sauce, heat a large casserole dish over a medium–high heat and after a few minutes, add the oil and lower the heat to medium. Add the onion, carrot and celery, season well with salt and pepper and cook for 8–10 minutes until soft. Add all but 2 cloves of the garlic, the oregano and bay leaves, stir and cook for another 3–4 minutes. Finally, add the sherry, olives, capers, pickled chillies, cinnamon, sugar and tomatoes, pour in 250ml (8fl oz) water and bring up to simmering point. Taste, adjust the seasoning and cook slowly for 30 minutes.

When you are ready to eat, preheat a hot grill (broiler) to medium and slice the polenta into long triangles. Drizzle with oil, sprinkle with grated cheese, if using, and grill (broil) for 10 minutes until golden on top and heated through.

While the polenta is grilling, warm the remaining olive oil in a wide, deep frying pan (skillet) and sauté the last of the garlic until pale golden. Stir in the greens and cook for a minute, then add 2–3 tablespoons of water and cover. Steam-fry for 4–5 minutes until tender.

Serve the polenta with the tomato sauce and greens, scattered with the pickled chillies.

CHIPOTLE CAULIFLOWER CHEESE & GREENS

WITH A CRISPY TOP

A gloriously smoky, Welsh rarebit-inspired cauliflower cheese, spiked with chipotles and scattered with a crispy golden crust of tortillas and grilled cheese. Leave out the tortilla crust for a lighter finish.

SERVES 4

1 large head of cauliflower or 2 medium-sized ones

250g (9oz) purple sprouting broccoli

FOR THE SAUCE

50g (2oz) butter

3 tbsp plain (all-purpose) flour

2 tsp English mustard powder

400ml (14fl oz) whole milk

200ml (7fl oz) amber ale or bitter

2 Chipotles en Adobo, plus extra to taste (page 234) (optional)

125g (4½oz) mature Cheddar cheese, Lincolnshire Poacher or any mature cheese scraps in the fridge, grated

2 tsp sweet smoked paprika

several good gratings of nutmeg

salt and pepper

FOR THE TORTILLA CRUST

75g (2½oz) blue or white tortilla chips, roughly crushed

75g (2½oz) mature Cheddar or Lincolnshire Poacher cheese, grated

Prepare a steamer to hold the vegetables. Cut away the tough outer leaves from the cauliflower but keep the young, tender ones. Trim the stalk and cut into thick coins. Cut the cauliflower into medium-size florets. Trim the broccoli and cut the stalks down the middle if they are thick and the broccoli in half lengths. Steam the broccoli for 6–7 minutes and the cauliflower for 4–5 minutes until just tender, adding the cauliflower leaves for the final minute of cooking. Once cooked, take away from the pan and leave to steam dry.

Preheat the oven to 200°C/180°C fan/400°F/gas 6. Melt the butter in a medium pan over a medium heat and, when foaming, stir in the flour and mustard powder and season with salt and pepper. Stir over a medium heat for 2–3 minutes, letting it bubble and toast. Add a good splash of milk and whisk until thick, then gradually add the rest of the milk, followed by the beer, whisking between additions to finish with a smooth sauce.

Bring up to heat and cook for a few minutes before stirring in the chipotles, cheese, paprika and nutmeg. Remove from the heat, check the seasoning and add more chipotle if you want a smokier, spicier sauce.

Put the vegetables in a large, shallow dish and stir in the cheese sauce. Combine the tortilla chips and Cheddar and scatter over the cauliflower. Bake for 25–30 minutes until golden and bubbling. Serve immediately as a side or with tortillas or slices of fresh bread and a crisp green salad as a main.

SPICY ANCHO MUSHROOM PASTA BAKE

Smoky, rounded, rich flavours from medium-spiced chillies, roast mushrooms, garlic, charred tomatoes and grilled cheese, this pasta bake is bold and robust, full of upfront, mouth-filling, umami-rich flavours, partly tempered by the sweet mellow undertones of the ancho and tomatoes, but then gently smoothed out by the soothing cheeses. My ten-year-old eats it by the trayful. It is a dish you will want to cook again and again, putting it on the table with a modest air, knowing that it will be a knockout. A red wine and a crisp green salad is a fine match.

SERVES 6

900g (2lb) mixed mushrooms (I use a mix of chestnut, portobello, shiitake)

2 large red onions, peeled and each cut into 8 wedges

120ml (4fl oz) olive oil, plus extra to drizzle

large handful of thyme

2 ancho chillies, about 30g (1oz), de-seeded

4 large ripe tomatoes, about 400g (14oz)

6 large garlic cloves, unpeeled

300g (10oz) large conchiglioni pasta

35g (1oz) sun-dried tomatoes

2–3 tsp Chipotles en Adobo (page 234)

1 tbsp red wine vinegar

1–2 tsp light brown soft sugar, to taste

2 balls of mozzarella, torn

60g (2oz) vegetarian pecorino or goat's Gouda, finely grated

salt and pepper

Preheat the oven to 220°C/200°C fan/425°F/gas 7. Line two baking trays with parchment paper.

Cut half the mushrooms into bite-size pieces. Finely chop or blitz the rest. Put the mushroom chunks and half the onions on one baking tray and the chopped mushrooms on another. Drizzle 4 tablespoons olive oil over each, season well and scatter with half the thyme. Roast in the oven for 40–45 minutes, tossing once or twice, until golden.

Briefly toast the ancho chilli pieces in a dry frying pan (skillet) set over a medium heat until fragrant. Try not to burn them! Pour over just enough boiling water to cover and soak for 10–15 minutes. In the same frying pan, dry-roast the rest of the onions, tomatoes and garlic over a high heat until blackened.

Meanwhile, cook the pasta in plenty of boiling water until al dente, drain and reserve the cooking water.

Once toasted, put the onion, garlic, rehydrated anchos, roast and sun-dried tomatoes into an upright blender and blitz for a minute. Add the rest of the thyme, 2 teaspoons of chipotle, 2 tablespoons of olive oil, the vinegar and 400ml (14fl oz) of the pasta water and blitz again to a smooth purée. Taste and season with plenty of salt and the brown sugar. The spice levels will mellow once baked.

Turn the oven down to 180°C/160°C fan/350°F/gas 4. Tip the mushrooms and pasta into a large baking dish and toss with the tomato-chilli sauce. Stir well and add more water if it looks dry. Check the seasoning, scatter over the cheeses and cook for 25–30 minutes until golden.

WHOLE ROAST CAULIFLOWER
WITH TEHUANO SAUCE, CRISPY CAPERS & ALMONDS

Do not be put off by the long list of ingredients in this utterly delicious sauce from the Isthmus region of Oaxaca, which balances classic Mexican spicing with mild chillies, sautéed fruit, capers and olives. It is mainly just an assembly job and then a building of the ingredients in a pan, and its flavour is unlike anything you will have tried before. Traditionally it is served with chicken or pork, but the sweet, caramelised notes of roast cauliflower are a great foil for the different elements of the sauce. Have a go, I don't think you'll regret it.

SERVES 2–4

2 guajillo chillies, de-stemmed and de-seeded, opened up like a book

4–5 tbsp mild olive oil or rapeseed (canola) oil, plus extra for the capers

1 large red onion, finely sliced

4 garlic cloves, chopped

1 small cinnamon stick

2 pinches of ground cloves

2 tbsp thyme or oregano

100g (3½oz) apple, cored and diced

100g (3½oz) banana, roughly chopped

45g (1½oz) raisins

1–2 tsp Chipotles en Adobo (page 234)

2–3 tsp brown sugar

1 x 400g (14oz) tin of plum tomatoes

1 tbsp red wine vinegar

60g (2oz) capers

60g (2oz) pitted green olives

salt and pepper

FOR THE CAULIFLOWER

1 large cauliflower

1 tsp paprika

1 tbsp olive oil

TO SERVE

30g (1oz) toasted almonds, chopped

handful of coriander (cilantro) leaves

Preheat the oven to 220°C/200°C fan/425°F/gas 7.

Place a small dry frying pan (skillet) over a medium heat and toast the chillies on both sides for a couple of seconds until slightly darkened, then pour over boiling water and soak for 10 minutes until soft.

Pour the oil into a large casserole dish and gently sauté the onion and garlic for 7–8 minutes until beginning to soften. Add the spices, herbs, apple, banana and half the raisins, turn up the heat a little and cook for another 7–8 minutes until the fruit is starting to caramelise.

Add the guajillo and chipotle together with the sugar, tomatoes, vinegar, half the capers and the olives. Pour in 250ml (8fl oz) water, season well and simmer for 15–20 minutes. Blitz to a smooth purée with a hand blender and then taste, adjusting the seasoning with salt, sugar and vinegar – it should taste sweet and savoury. At this stage you can leave the sauce for up to 3 days and its flavour will improve in the fridge.

When you are ready to eat, trim the cauliflower stem so it sits flat in the dish and pull back the leaves to expose the head. Rub all over with the paprika and oil and season. Nestle the cauliflower in the sauce, cover and roast for 35–40 minutes before removing the lid and roasting for another 15 minutes, when the cauliflower should be tender.

Fry the remaining capers and raisins in hot oil until they are crisp and golden. Serve the cauliflower and its sauce, sprinkled with the capers, raisins, almonds and coriander.

CHILE NON CARNE

I first developed this recipe when a *Guardian* reader begged me for a meat-free version of the famous Tex-Mex dish. I confess that I used to be a bit snotty about chile con carne when I first started cooking Mexican food: I was just so passionate about people discovering what real Mexican was like when Tex-Mex had so stolen the show! Those days are long gone – who doesn't love a great chile? This is a delicious, warming, wonderful bowl of vegetable chile non carne.

SERVES 6–8

700g (1½lb) sweet potatoes, peeled and cut into 3cm (1¼ inch) chunks

500g (1lb 2oz) parsnip or celeriac (celery root), peeled and cut into 3cm (1¼ inch) chunks

6 tbsp olive or rapeseed (canola) oil

2 chipotle chillies, de-seeded and opened like a book

1 ancho chilli, de-seeded and opened like a book

2 onions, chopped

3 garlic cloves, roughly chopped

2 tsp ground cumin

1 tsp ground coriander

1 tsp ground cinnamon

1 heaped tsp dried oregano

2 x 400g (14oz) tins of black beans, drained and rinsed

2 x 400g (14oz) tins of plum tomatoes

1–2 tbsp light brown soft sugar, to taste

30g (1oz) 70% cocoa dark (bittersweet) chocolate, grated

salt and pepper

TO SERVE

coriander (cilantro) leaves

Guacamole (page 62)

rice (pages 82–83)

salsas (pages 226–233)

tortillas (pages 245–246)

sour cream or plant-based sour cream

Preheat the oven to 220°C/200°C fan/425°F/gas 7. Put the sweet potatoes and parsnip or celeriac on a baking tray, drizzle over half the oil and season generously. Toss everything together with your hands, spread out and roast for 30–35 minutes until the veg is crisp around the edges and tender in the middle.

Toast the dried chillies in a preheated, small, dry frying pan (skillet) for 30–40 seconds each side (page 244), then cover with boiling water and leave to hydrate for 10–15 minutes.

Meanwhile, warm the remaining oil in a large saucepan over a medium heat and fry the onions with a big pinch of salt for 10 minutes until they begin to soften. Add the garlic and cook for another 3 minutes or so until soft. Drain the chillies, chop them finely, then add half to the onions, along with the spices and oregano. Fry for a minute, then add the beans, tomatoes, sugar and chocolate, then fill up the tomato tin with hot water and add to the pan.

Bring to the boil, then simmer for 15 minutes until reduced. Stir in the roasted vegetables and taste. If you want more spice, add the remaining chillies. Simmer for another 15 minutes until the sauce has thickened. Check the seasoning, then sprinkle over the coriander and serve with guacamole, rice, salsas, tortillas and sour cream. And maybe some lager and great tequila.

MEXICAN PIZZAS
WITH AUBERGINE, MOZZARELLA & ROAST CHERRY TOMATOES

Tlayudas [clah-yoo-dahs] are Mexican-style pizzas cooked over charcoal grills late at night in Oaxaca. There the dough is made with corn, but here I make simple wheat tortillas using delicious heritage flours, that puff up in a wildly energetic manner. Finish them off under a hot grill until the cheese is melted and bubbling. Incredibly good party food that will make you look like a kitchen wizard.

SERVES 4–6

3 large aubergines (eggplants)

400g (14oz) mixed small tomatoes

1–2 red chillies

12 spring onions (scallions)

5 garlic cloves, unpeeled

3 tbsp olive oil

1½ tbsp good cider or red wine vinegar

1 tsp Mexican oregano

home-made flour tortillas (page 245) or shop-bought

2 balls of mozzarella, torn into pieces

60g (2oz) vegetarian pecorino or hard goat's cheese, grated

salt and pepper

TO SERVE

Habanero Oil (page 236) or other chilli oil

small handful of coriander (cilantro) leaves

large handful of rocket (arugula)

Heat up the barbecue, a griddle pan or preheat the grill (broiler) to its highest setting.

Grill/griddle (broil) the aubergine, tomatoes, chillies, spring onions and garlic over the barbecue or in a hot griddle pan. Alternatively, roast the aubergines over a gas flame or grill in a very hot oven: de-stalk, cut into quarters and spread out on a foil-lined baking tray with the other ingredients. Turn the ingredients as they grill: the garlic and spring onions will be tender after about 6–8 minutes; the tomatoes and chillies after about 15 minutes; the aubergine after 20–25 minutes.

Slip the skins off the garlic and de-stalk the chillies. Chop with ½ teaspoon of salt then squash firmly with the flat of your knife to a rough purée. Scrape into a bowl and mix with the oil, vinegar and oregano.

Empty the tomatoes into a large mixing bowl. Roughly chop the spring onions and add half to the tomatoes, leaving the rest for the garnish. De-stalk the aubergine and roughly chop. Scoop into the bowl, pour over the sauce and gently turn to coat. Taste and adjust the seasoning and balance of vinegar to your liking.

Transfer the tortillas to baking sheets and top with some of the aubergine mix, a scattering of the spring onions and the cheeses. Pop under a hot grill until the cheese has melted. Drizzle with chilli oil and serve scattered with coriander and rocket.

OTHER TLAYUDA TOPPINGS I LIKE

Roast Beets (page 156) with crumbled goat's cheese, chimichurri & rocket (arugula)

Mushrooms 'al Ajillo' (page 120) with grated pecorino/hard sheep's cheese and sweetcorn purée

Grilled courgettes (zucchini) and their flowers with mozzarella, chilli oil & mint

Roast squash, roast cherry tomatoes & Ajillo Oil (page 236)

CHOCOLATE, VANILLA & OTHER STORIES

Chocolate and vanilla – both from Mexico, both delicious. One is haunting, fleeting in nature, the other bold, assertive and multifaceted with its many flavour profiles. I find it wondrous that these two ingredients are among the most coveted in the world.

This chapter is a celebration of puddings and cakes scented and folded through with vanilla and chocolate. Buy a bottle of good tequila and marvel at how it complements the chocolate in a hot chocolate sauce poured over vanilla ice cream, or in my molten chocolate and ancho cake. This chapter is also a revelry of recipes using some of Mexico's tropical fruits. A recipe remembering the sweetest pineapples I have tasted, here baked in a tarte Tatin; blood oranges blitzed with tequila and Campari to make the naughtiest, most glamorous finish to a meal; and vanilla-scented cheesecakes from outside the San Juan market, cooked in the Basque style but made Mexican with an intense fruit jam. I celebrate the coconut trees of the Mexican Riviera, with a sticky, fudgy coconut tart, and I honour Spain's culinary influence on Mexico's pastry scene with its love of flan and churros.

For the sweet-toothed, this is an exuberant romp through a world of Mexican-inspired sweet treats.

VANILLA ICE CREAM
WITH HOT CHOCOLATE SAUCE

Vanilla and chocolate: two of the most expensive ingredients in the world and both originating in Mexico. This simple pudding is one that I make more than any other because it needs very little work and because it is insanely, decadently, deliriously good. The brittle can be made in advance and makes for an addictive, salty, nutty top, though you can leave it out if you want. The combination of the mood elevating chocolate and sun-soaked agave tequila with the euphoric buzz that pair induces, means that invariably this pudding disappears faster than it might first seem possible – it really is hard to beat!

SERVES 6-ISH

1–2 tubs of vanilla ice cream

FOR THE CHOCOLATE SAUCE

200g (7oz) dark (bittersweet) raw chocolate (your favourite one)

3–4 tbsp unaged tequila (blanco) (must be 100% agave)

60ml (2fl oz) double (heavy) cream

100ml (3½fl oz) whole milk

scrunch of sea salt

1 heaped tbsp golden (light corn) syrup

FOR THE SALTED PEANUT-SESAME BRITTLE (OPTIONAL)

70g (2½oz) sesame seeds

100g (3½oz) roasted peanuts, roughly chopped

40g (1½oz) butter

120g (4½oz) sugar

100g (3½oz) golden (light corn) syrup

1 tsp sea salt flakes

COOK'S NOTES This makes a crumbly brittle you can either cut into shards or chop up like a praline. Pre-toasting the seeds and peanuts is really worth it for the flavour. It will last for a week in an airtight container.

Preheat the oven to 180°C/160°C fan/350°F/gas 4.

If you are making the brittle, line a baking tray with parchment paper and spread both the sesame seeds and chopped peanuts out on the tray. Roast for 10–15 minutes, checking halfway through cooking to shake the tray. You want the nuts and seeds to be evenly roasted and not to catch.

In a small pan, combine the butter, sugar and golden syrup and stir over a medium heat. Once the mixture starts to bubble, remove from the heat. Remove the peanuts and sesame from the oven and add to the pan. Pour the combined mixture straight onto the warm baking tray and parchment paper (the warmth of the tray will help to keep the mixture more pliable). Try to spread the mixture as thinly as possible.

Put the tray back in the oven and cook for another 15 minutes. Remove from the oven, sprinkle with the flaked sea salt and leave to cool completely before breaking the brittle into shards.

When you are ready to eat, get the ice cream out of the freezer to thaw. Melt the chocolate sauce ingredients together in a small saucepan and taste, adding more tequila, if you feel it warrants, or more milk if the sauce needs thinning down. Serve the ice cream, chocolate sauce and brittle all at the table for people to help themselves.

PINEAPPLE TARTE TATIN
WITH RUM CREAM

A deep, rich caramel envelopes the pineapple in this unashamedly wanton tarte Tatin. Layer upon layer of exotic spice notes from the cinnamon and anise, with lime zest adding fresh, floral citrus. The boozy rum cream follows swiftly for a heady assault. This is not a pudding to be messed with – serve at the end of a fat lunch and sink back in your chair afterwards with a small glass of mezcal.

SERVES 8–10

325g (11½oz) block of pre-rolled puff pastry

plain (all-purpose) flour, for dusting

1 pineapple (about 600g/1¼lb)

200g (7oz) caster (superfine) sugar

60g (2oz) unsalted butter

1 tsp vanilla extract

1 cinnamon stick

2 star anise

pinch of salt

zest of 1 lime, to serve

FOR THE RUM CREAM

250ml (8fl oz) double (heavy) cream

4 tbsp icing (confectioners') sugar

2–3 tbsp rum

Preheat the oven to 200°C/180°C fan/400°F/gas 6.

Roll out the pastry to a 3mm (⅛ inch) thickness, then cut to the size of your ovenproof frying pan (approx. 24cm/9½ inches). Place on a floured plate and return to the fridge.

Peel the pineapple, cut in half or quarters and remove the core. Cut into sliced 1cm (½ inch) thick.

Make the caramel next. Pour the caster sugar into a wide pan and place over a medium heat. Cook for 6–9 minutes, occasionally swirling the pan (not stirring) until the sugar has melted and is golden amber. Add the pineapple, butter, vanilla, spices and salt and simmer for 6–8 minutes, basting and turning each slice in the sauce every few minutes. The sugar may clump but it will melt again.

Take off the heat and arrange the pineapple slices so they're overlapping and evenly covering the bottom of the pan. Cover with the puff pastry, tucking it in at the edges, and prick the top all over with a fork. Bake for 20–25 minutes until the pastry is deep golden and crisp.

While the tart is in the oven, transfer the cream, sugar and rum to a large bowl and whip until you have soft peaks. Chill until you're ready to serve.

Leave the tart to cool for 5 minutes, then invert onto a serving dish and sprinkle with lime zest. Serve with the rum cream.

ALTERNATIVE

CHARGRILLED PINEAPPLE WITH RUM CREAM

Remove the pineapple skin and slice into 8–10 wedges. In a pan, bring all the caramel ingredients to the boil and simmer for 5 minutes. Set aside. Char the pineapple for 10–12 minutes on a barbecue/griddle on all sides. Lay on a serving dish and pour over the syrup. Serve with the rum cream and lime.

STICKY COCONUT TART
WITH ORANGE & LIME

This deliciously chewy, orange and lime-scented coconut tart reminds me of sunny travels along the Caribbean coast of Mexico, where coconut trees abound as well as Seville orange trees, first brought to the continent by the Spanish. It is common to use a mixture of fresh orange and lime juice to replicate the flavours of the Seville orange in this part of the world. It works beautifully in this fudgy tart which I like to eat with thick cream or Greek yoghurt. I use organic spelt flour and ground almonds for a lower gluten finish.

SERVES 8

3 eggs

180g (6½oz) soft brown sugar

zest and juice of 2 limes

zest and juice of large orange

375ml (12½fl oz) double (heavy) cream, plus extra to serve

240g (8½oz) unsweetened coconut, dessicated or flaked and blitzed fine

large pinch of sea salt

FOR THE PASTRY

250g (9oz) white spelt flour

100g (3½oz) ground almonds

100g (3½oz) icing (confectioners') sugar

200g (7oz) fridge-cold unsalted butter, cut into dice

few pinches of fine sea salt

2 eggs, separated

Preheat the oven to 180°C/160°C fan/350°F/gas 4 and butter a 24–25cm (9½–10 inch) tart case.

To make the pastry, empty the flour, almonds, sugar, butter and salt into a food processor and blitz briefly to get fine breadcrumbs. Add the yolks and pulse a few times. Open the lid and feel the mixture. If it just about comes together, empty out onto a cold work surface. If it is not sticking together, add 1–2 teaspoons of iced water and pulse a few times more. Work the pastry as little as possible and don't worry if it still looks a little crumbly.

Bring together the pastry into a ball deftly with your hands. Roughly flatten, wrap in cling film (plastic wrap) and rest in the fridge for 15 minutes. Once it has cooled down, roughly grate as much as you need to line the tart tin, flattening it out around the tin and rolling it smooth with a small glass. Freeze for 15 minutes before filling with parchment and baking beans. Bake for 15–20 minutes. Remove the baking beans, brush the pastry case with some of the egg white (you can keep the rest to add to an omelette or to make financiers) and return to the oven for a final 5 minutes until pale golden.

While the pastry is doing its thing empty the eggs and brown sugar into an electric mixer and beat on high speed for a few minutes until light and fluffy. Add the citrus zest and juices, the cream, coconut and salt. Once the pastry case is cooked, pour in the coconut filling and bake for about 45 minutes until the tart has risen and is looking golden and tempting. Cool to room temperature and serve with cream and small glasses of reposado tequila.

MINI LIME BASQUE CHEESECAKES
WITH CHERRY COMPOTE

San Juan is an amazing food market in Mexico City that I would often visit to find a particular ingredient or just when I was homesick. Outside one of the entrances, and next door to a celebrated Veracruzan street-food stand, was a wonderfully traditional, wood-panelled coffee shop that was famous for their mini cheesecakes, served with a spoonful of jam nestled inside each one. I became obsessed with them long before I clocked their Basque origins. Here I serve them with a home-made cinnamon-scented cherry compote on the side, it provides a wondrous burst of sweet, sharp fruit against the smooth lime-scented cream.

MAKES 12 CHEESECAKES

FOR THE CHEESECAKES

360g (13oz) cream cheese

90g (3oz) caster (superfine) sugar

100g (3½oz) double (heavy) cream

1½ tsp vanilla extract

¼ tsp fine sea salt

zest of 1 lime

2 eggs

20g (¾oz) cornflour (cornstarch)

FOR THE CHERRY COMPOTE

400g (14oz) cherries, halved and stoned (or frozen cherries, defrosted)

120g (4½oz) caster (superfine) sugar

zest and juice of 1 lime

1 cinnamon stick

Preheat the oven to 220°C/200°C fan/425°F/gas 7. Line a muffin tin or cupcake tray with 12 large paper muffin cases (the largest size you can buy or make your own, using 18cm/7 inch square sheets of parchment paper, though that's admittedly a slightly fiddly job).

Using an electric hand mixer, beat the cream cheese and sugar until smooth. Add the cream, vanilla, salt and lime zest and beat again until smooth and fluffy, about 1 minute. Next, crack in the eggs one at a time, mixing the first one in before adding the following one. Lastly, sift in the cornflour and mix it very briefly until just incorporated.

Spoon the mixture into each case. Bake in the middle of the oven for 25–30 minutes.

While the cheesecakes are cooking, make the compote. Add the cherries, sugar, lime zest and cinnamon stick to a small saucepan over a medium heat. If using fresh cherries, add 2 tablespoons of water to the pan. Cook for 8–10 minutes until the cherries lose their shape and a syrupy sauce is formed. Turn off the heat, remove the cinnamon stick and add the lime juice.

Check the cheesecakes are dark golden on top – they need to start to look burnt. Once cooked, remove and place on a rack to cool. Serve the cheesecakes with the compote on the side.

ORANGE RICOTTA DOUGHNUTS
WITH HIBISCUS SUGAR

These light, ethereal, Italian-inspired doughnuts are fragrant with the scent of orange and look gorgeous tossed in the violet-coloured hibiscus sugar. They are a total treat for the end of a meal – a sure way to win in any popularity stakes.

MAKES 12 DOUGHNUTS

2 eggs

80g (3oz) caster (superfine) sugar

zest of 1 orange

250g (9oz) ricotta

115g (4oz) plain (all-purpose) flour

2 tsp baking powder

¼ tsp salt

10g (¼oz) dried hibiscus flowers

vegetable or sunflower oil, for frying

Whisk the eggs in a bowl, then whisk in 40g (1½oz) of sugar and the orange zest. Add the ricotta and fold gently to combine – don't overmix – you need to keep some of the lumps to make the dough hold. In another bowl, whisk together the flour, baking powder and salt, then fold into the ricotta mixture.

Blitz the hibiscus flowers to a fine powder in a small food processor and then sift into a small bowl. Mix them with the remaining 40g (1½oz) of sugar and set aside.

Put a deep pan over a medium heat and pour in enough oil to come 4cm (1½ inches) up the sides. Warm to 160–170°C (320–340°F). A sugar thermometer is a big help here or test the dough by dropping in a little to see if it sizzles and floats.

Using two tablespoons, carefully drop tablespoons of the batter into the oil and fry for 2–3 minutes until golden on all sides. They should turn themselves over after a minute or so but if not, turn with a slotted spoon.

Using the same slotted spoon, lift out the doughnuts when they are golden and transfer to a plate lined with kitchen paper. Repeat with the remaining batter.

Once all the doughnuts are cooked, toss in the hibiscus sugar and serve at once. These invariably vanish moments after they have been tossed in the sugar but if in doubt, they are best eaten straight away in any case. You can keep warm in an oven if necessary.

CHURROS

WITH DARK CHOCOLATE SAUCE

These churros are the classic Mexican ones, naturally free of eggs or dairy. Although my children love them with dulce de leche, I love them with chocolate every time, particularly when a dash or two of a good tequila has been added to the mix. There is little as pleasing as the heady taste of melted chocolate and tequila at the end of an evening.

MAKES 12–14 CHURROS, DEPENDING ON THEIR LENGTHS

2 tbsp olive oil

½ tsp fine sea salt

140g (5oz) white spelt flour

1 tsp baking powder

dash of vanilla extract

vegetable or sunflower oil, for frying

FOR THE CINNAMON SUGAR

100g (3½oz) caster (superfine) sugar

1 tsp ground cinnamon

FOR THE CHOCOLATE SAUCE

250g (9oz) dark (bittersweet) chocolate, roughly chopped

2 tbsp golden (light corn) syrup

½ x 400ml (14fl oz) tin of coconut milk

1–2 tbsp blanco tequila (optional)

pinch of sea salt

COOK'S NOTE The sauce can be kept in the fridge for a week but it will solidify, so loosen with a dash of coconut milk or water when reheating.

To make the cinnamon sugar, mix the sugar and cinnamon together in a shallow bowl and set aside.

Put the chocolate in a heavy-based pan with the golden syrup. Give the tin of coconut milk a good shake before opening and adding 200ml (7fl oz) to the pan. Stir continuously over a low heat to melt the chocolate, being careful not to let it burn. Once melted, remove from the heat and stir in the tequila, if using. Season with a pinch of sea salt.

Heat 300ml (10½fl oz) water, the olive oil and salt in a medium saucepan until it has just reached simmering point. Tip in the flour, baking powder and vanilla and quickly beat together with a wooden spoon until it forms a smooth ball on the side of the pan. Transfer the dough to a piping bag with an 8mm (⅓ inch) star-tip nozzle. Set aside while the oil heats.

Heat about 6cm (2–3 inches) of oil in a small saucepan, wok or deep frying pan (skillet). You need it over a medium heat and for the oil to reach about 170°C (340°F), or until it takes 20 seconds for a small cube of bread to turn golden. If the oil is too hot, the dough will burn before it is fully cooked; too cold, and the churros will be greasy.

Pipe the dough into the oil, snipping the dough at finger lengths with scissors, close to the oil surface to avoid splashing. Fry in batches of around four at a time for a few minutes each side until crisp and golden, rolling occasionally to brown all the sides. Remove to drain on a plate lined with kitchen paper. Roll in the cinnamon sugar and serve hot with the chocolate sauce.

TAMARIND CRÈME BRÛLÉE

Crème brûlée is a popular pudding in Mexico thanks to the country's years under French rule. Tamarind is used all over Mexico in salsas and savoury saces, but is also popular in sweets and cocktails with its decidedly more-ish sweet-and-sour flavour. Panela is a rich, nutty-tasting unrefined brown sugar that matches these sour notes beautifully, or use light muscovado in its place. The combination of the dark sugar and the sour, fruity tamarind is wonderful and stains the cream a pale shade of tangerine under the irresistible crunch of the sugar crust.

SERVES 6–8

425ml (15fl oz) double (heavy) cream

1½ tsp vanilla extract

2½ tbsp tamarind paste (page 245)

6 egg yolks

45g (1½oz) panela or muscovado sugar

caster (superfine) sugar, to serve

Put the cream, vanilla and tamarind into a heavy-bottomed saucepan and put over a medium heat. Bring the cream to simmering point but remove from the heat before it boils.

Preheat the oven to 170°C/150°C fan/325°F/gas 3.

Whisk the egg yolks with the sugar until the eggs are fluffy. Whisk in the warm cream. Now taste the mixture and add more tamarind if it needs it – no pulp is ever the same. Pour this mixture into an ovenproof serving dish and lay the dish in a deeper roasting tray. Fill this with enough water to come halfway up the serving dish and bake in the oven for 25–35 minutes until the cream has just set. Remove from the oven and from the roasting dish and leave to cool. Refrigerate overnight to set.

The next day, either heat a grill (broiler) to its highest setting or use a cook's blowtorch (which is much easier). Sprinkle a generous layer of caster sugar over the cream to a depth of 3–4mm (¼ inch). Using the grill or a blowtorch, grill (broil) the sugar until it has melted into a smooth, glassy top coat. Return to the fridge, preferably a few hours before you are ready to eat. Serve at the table with a big spoon for people to crack the crunchy sugar layer.

COOK'S NOTES Making tamarind pulp from the pods takes a few minutes and its flavour is so much better than the expensive jars that it is well worth it, especially in a pudding as luxurious as this. See page 245 for the method.

MOLTEN DARK CHOCOLATE ANCHO CAKE

This deliriously gooey chocolate cake was inspired by a pudding I tried in Mexico City, steeped with the sweet notes of ancho chilli. The twice-baked method is one from St. JOHN's restaurant, recently given a renaissance by the wonderful pastry chef Ravneet Gill – it is foolproof and ensures a squidgy molten core.

SERVES 8–10

240g (8½oz) unsalted butter, plus extra for greasing

7 eggs, separated

260g (9oz) caster (superfine) sugar

80g (3oz) blanched hazelnuts (filberts)

240g (8½oz) dark (bittersweet) chocolate

1 ancho chilli, stem and seeds discarded, or 10g (¼oz) ancho flakes, placed in boiling hot water

2 tbsp blanco or reposado tequila

1 tsp vanilla extract

25g (1oz) cocoa powder

¼ tsp ground cinnamon

large pinch of salt

Preheat the oven to 190°C/170°C fan/375°F/gas 5 and grease a 23cm (9 inch) springform cake tin with butter and line with parchment paper.

Put the egg yolks in the bowl of a mixer with the sugar and beat for a few minutes until the yolks have tripled in volume. Empty the nuts onto a baking (cookie) sheet and toast in the oven for 5–10 minutes until pale golden. Do put on a timer – there is nothing more irritating than burning nuts!

Meanwhile, put the chocolate and butter in a bain-marie over a low-ish heat. Drain the chilli, pound to a paste with a pestle and mortar or chopping knife, and add to the chocolate with the tequilla and vanilla. Stir a few times until melted, about 5–10 minutes. If the chocolate splits, don't worry, it will come back when you add the eggs.

In a small grinder, blitz the nuts with the cocoa powder, cinnamon and salt and set aside. Beat the egg whites with an electric whisk to soft peaks. Gradually pour the melted chocolate into the yolks, using a stick blender to thoroughly combine. Fold in the nuts, followed by the whites, in three stages.

Empty half the mixture into the prepared tin and smooth the top. Bake for 20–25 minutes until risen and a metal skewer inserted into the centre comes out clean. Rest for 10 minutes. You can keep the cake overnight and finish the baking the next day or cool for 1 hour and carry on.

Turn the oven up to 210°C/190°C fan/425°F/gas 7. Pour the rest of the mixture onto the cake and smooth, leaving a border around the edges. Bake for 12–15 minutes until a light crust has formed on top. Cool for 10 minutes, then tuck in. It lasts well for up to 3 days stored at room temperature or in the fridge, where the top becomes mousse-like.

PUMPKIN SEED & CHOCOLATE CAKE

I came across this cake watching videos of Rick Bayliss. It is a wonderfully nutty cake adapted here with sea salt, cinnamon and rum, for a rich, sophisticated, after-dinner cake. The grown-up flavour of the rum is a great match for the nuances of good-quality dark chocolate so use a good one if you can. Serve with softly whipped cream and you have a corker of a pudding. Or replace the rum with a teaspoon of vanilla extract for a delicious tea cake.

SERVES 8–10

250g (9oz) pumpkin seeds

115g (4oz) unsalted butter, room temperature, plus extra for greasing

2 tbsp Demerara sugar

200g (7oz) golden caster (superfine) sugar

100g (3½oz) 70% cocoa dark (bittersweet) chocolate, roughly chopped

1 tbsp dark rum

3 eggs

60g (2oz) white spelt or gluten-free flour

½ tsp baking powder

1 tsp ground cinnamon

zest of 1 orange

3 tsp icing (confectioners') sugar

Preheat the oven to 180°C/160°C fan/350°F/gas 4.

Toast the pumpkin seeds in a large wide frying pan (skillet), doing it in two batches if you need to, to allow the pumpkin seeds to be spread out in one layer. Toast them until they turn pale golden, with some of them popping energetically as they colour. Reserve 50g (2oz) of pumpkin seeds and transfer the rest to a food processor, allowing them to cool while you prepare the cake tin.

Generously butter a 20cm (8 inch) round tin and line the bottom with a round of parchment paper. Now, butter the parchment paper and sprinkle it with the Demerara sugar and the 50g (2oz) reserved pumpkin seeds. Set aside.

Add the caster sugar to the pumpkin seeds in the food processor. Whizz together until the texture resembles wet sand. Add the chocolate and rum and pulse-blitz for a few seconds. Now add the butter and eggs and pulse until combined.

In a separate bowl, mix together the flour, baking powder, cinnamon and orange zest. Add these to the food processor and pulse briefly until just combined, trying not to overwork the batter or it will become heavy.

Scrape the mixture into the prepared tin and bake for 40 minutes, or until a skewer inserted in the centre pulls out clean.

Leave to cool before removing from the tin and serving with a dusting of sifted icing sugar. This is lovely with crème fraîche, softly whipped double (heavy) cream or Greek yoghurt.

INDIVIDUAL VANILLA FLANS

WITH ESPRESSO SAUCE

Flan is usually far too sweet or far too delicious! Carolyn Lum is 12 years at Wahaca and counting, and a woman with an extraordinary palate; she and I were once driven an hour across the Yucatan by the most generous host Ricardo Ugalde (Mexican, naturally) to try the region's most famous one. He couldn't quite believe it when, having shared the first flan (we had already had an extremely large breakfast and an even bigger lunch) we promptly ordered two more. This rich, coffee-fuelled version is inspired by that flan, and the Mexicans' love of affogato. The bitter dark notes of the boozy espresso give a cheeky jolt to the otherwise beautifully cool vanilla cream.

SERVES 6

4 eggs plus 2 egg yolks

120g (4½oz) caster (superfine) sugar

500ml (17fl oz) double (heavy) cream

300ml (10½fl oz) whole milk

1 tsp vanilla extract

FOR THE COFFEE CARAMEL

150g (5oz) caster (superfine) sugar

3 tbsp reposado tequila (optional)

3 tbsp strong filtered/espresso coffee

To make the coffee caramel, put the sugar with 3 tablespoons of water in a heavy-bottomed pan and put over a medium heat. Meanwhile, put the tequila (or 3 tablespoons water) and coffee in a cup together, ready for the caramel. Carefully melt the sugar, without stirring, and then turn up the heat to simmer gently and allow to caramelise, swirling to distribute the sugar evenly as patches darken in colour. It will take about 10–12 minutes to caramelise the sugar depending on the heat; the colour should be a deep maple brown and smell delicious, but if it turns too dark, it will end up burning. When you think the caramel looks right, turn the heat right down, pour in the coffee (be careful, it will splutter) and whisk until the caramel is smooth. Divide the caramel among eight ovenproof pots or dariole moulds and set aside somewhere cool to set.

Preheat the oven to 130°C/110°C fan/275°F/gas 1.

To make the flan, whisk the eggs, yolks and sugar together, then whisk in the cream, milk and vanilla. Put the flan moulds in a baking tray and fill each with about 150ml (5fl oz) of the mix. Put the tray in the oven and fill with enough boiling water to come halfway up the moulds. Bake until just set, about 40–45 minutes. The flans will wobble gently but they should hold their shape – they will set in the fridge later. Cool for 30 minutes before refrigerating for at least 4 hours or overnight. Turn upside down to release the flans to serve.

LIME POSSET
WITH BERRIES & OAT-COCONUT SHARDS

The two quickest recipes in this book: a posset with zingy lime instead of lemon and the most impossibly delicious toasted coconut and oat shards served on the side, which are so irresistible that I can win over the grumpiest of children if I throw a tray of these into the oven. Toasted, caramelised coconut is a thing in Mexico – it has my mouth watering every time.

SERVES 6

150g (5oz) blackberries

100ml (3½fl oz) lime juice (from approx. 4 juicy limes), plus their zest

600ml (21oz) double (heavy) cream

120g (4½oz) caster (superfine) sugar, plus extra to serve

2 tbsp tequila (optional)

FOR THE OAT-COCONUT SHARDS

100g (3½oz) butter

100g (3½oz) soft brown sugar

100g (3½oz) desiccated (dried shredded) coconut

100g (3½oz) oats

generous pinch of salt

Preheat the oven to 180°C/160°C fan/350°F/gas 4 and line a baking tray with parchment paper.

Place the blackberries in a bowl and scatter with half the lime zest.

Pour the cream and 100g (3½oz) sugar into a deep pan, place over a medium heat and bring to a simmer, stirring, until the sugar has dissolved. As soon as you see the first boiling bubbles appear around the edge, take off the heat and stir in all the lime juice and the rest of the lime zest. Immediately pour into six small glasses or bowls, allow to cool, then place in the fridge for at least 3 hours to firm up. You can also make them a couple of days ahead.

To make the oat crumble, melt the butter and brown sugar together in a pan. Meanwhile, blitz the coconut and oats in a food processor with a generous pinch of salt to fine breadcrumbs. Transfer to a bowl and mix in the butter thoroughly. Transfer to the tray and push down firmly so it's flat and tightly packed. Roll out as thinly as possible with a clean jam jar. Cook in the oven for 10–12 minutes or until golden. Once cool, break into shards.

Sprinkle the remaining sugar and the tequila, if using, over the blackberries. Leave to macerate for 30 minutes somewhere cool. Serve the possets with the blackberries spooned over and with shards of the oat-coconut crumble.

COOK'S NOTES The crumbly oat shards make a fine granola. Possibly less healthy than other ones around, but still exceedingly good with Greek yoghurt and the Chia, Raspberry & Hibiscus Jam on page 54.

TEQUILA & ORANGE CAMPARI SORBETS

A grown-up pudding to serve for people you really love, this is a stunning way to round off a rich meal and a good one if you want people dancing on the tables. Make the recipe without the booze and replace it with a teaspoon of good-quality cider vinegar if you are giving this to people who don't drink. The blood oranges stain the sorbet a brilliant colour, but of course it works well with any orange, or lemon for that matter!

SERVES 8 DEPENDING ON ORANGE SIZE (VO)

8 blood oranges (350ml/12fl oz blood orange juice and pulp combined)

250g (9oz) caster (superfine) sugar

2 tbsp mint, stalks and leaves

100ml (3½fl oz) lime juice

75ml (2½4fl oz) tequila

25ml (¾fl oz) Campari

mezcal (optional)

To prepare the frozen blood oranges, cut the top third off each orange and carefully juice both parts. Use a spoon to hollow out the oranges, being careful not to pierce the skin. Slice a very small amount off the bottom of each orange so that it will sit still without rolling around (behave!). Arrange cut side up on a small tray, keeping the lids separate, and freeze while you make the sorbet.

To make the sorbet, put 350ml (12fl oz) of the juice and pulp into saucepan with the sugar and 300ml (10½fl oz) water. Bring to simmering point and cook gently for 5–10 minutes until the sugar has melted. Turn off the heat, add the mint and lime juice, and steep for 15 minutes. Once cooled, stir in the tequila and Campari.

Now, strain into an ice-cream machine or into a freezable container and stir-freeze by hand or in the machine. Once the sorbet is soft and churned, spoon or pipe the sorbet back into the frozen oranges, one by one, only taking them out when you need them and putting them back in as you fill them.

Serve the oranges on pretty serving plates with a bottle of mezcal plonked on the table. A drizzle of smoky mezcal is incredible over this sorbet.

COCONUT & LIME RICE PUDDING

The rice pudding served in British schools through the generations has been the stuff of nightmares for many. This Mexican version, served chilled, is scented with citrus, cinnamon and other delights. Roberto Solis, the wonderful chef from Merida, used to make a delicately flavoured one topped with spoonfuls of caramelised brandy apples. It was spectacular! The key is not to make it too sweet, to chill it thoroughly and to stir enough cream or yoghurt through to loosen it to a texture of velvet – I hope it will be a revelation.

SERVES 6–8

200g (7oz) pudding rice

1 cinnamon stick

1 vanilla pod or 1 tsp vanilla extract

600ml (21fl oz) coconut or whole milk

80g (3oz) light brown sugar

zest and juice of 2 juicy limes

TO SERVE

2 ripe mangoes

zest and juice of 1 lime

200g (7oz) crème fraîche
or coconut yoghurt

few pinches of ground cinnamon

Wash the rice in cold water, then drain through a sieve. Put into a heavy-bottomed saucepan, pour in 650ml (22fl oz) cold water and add the cinnamon stick and vanilla pod, if using. Bring to the boil. Cover the pan, turn the heat down and cook slowly for 15 minutes or until the rice is tender. Stir from time to time so that the rice doesn't stick to the pan. Most of the water should have been absorbed by the time the rice is cooked but if not, drain the remnants.

Remove the cinnamon stick and the vanilla pod and, using a sharp knife, open up the pod and scrape the seeds into the saucepan with the rice. Add the milk, sugar, lime zest and vanilla extract, if you are using it instead of the pod, and cook gently for a further 8–10 minutes until the rice is fairly thick and creamy. Stir in the lime juice.

Remove from the heat and decant into a container. Once cool, refrigerate for at least 4 hours or overnight.

When you are ready to eat, peel the mangoes, cut into cubes and stir through the zest and juice of the lime. Mix enough crème fraîche or coconut yoghurt through the rice pudding to loosen (it should be light and drop off a spoon like a good risotto) and serve dusted with a pinch or two of cinnamon and the mango.

POMEGRANATE & LIME JELLIES

I am always flooded with a child-like pleasure when I pass the jelly carts trundling around Oaxaca's historic centre, with multicoloured double or triple-layered jellies of various flavours stacked up and arranged in beautiful patterns. At home I make them with seasonal fruits so that they taste as good as they look. They make a great end to dinner as they are not too rich and slip down deliciously. Do, of course, use bought pomegranate juice instead of fresh if you prefer, or experiment with layers – passion fruit, hibiscus and elderflower are all great flavours.

MAKES 4 JELLIES (VO)

vegetable oil (optional)

500g (1lb 2 oz) pomegranate seeds from approx. 2 large pomegranates (or 350ml/12fl oz pomegranate juice)

40g (1½oz) caster (superfine) sugar

45ml (1½fl oz) lime juice

2½ tbsp agar flakes or vege-gel

Rub the insides of four jelly or dariole moulds with a light, flavourless vegetable oil or simply set in some small pretty glasses, in which case there is no need for oiling.

Roll the pomegranates along the work surface, pushing down on them hard to 'pop' out the seeds. Break open one pomegranate at a time over a large bowl, with a second bowl at hand for the discards. Tease the seeds out of the fruit into the first bowl, discarding the skin and bitter white pith as you do into the second. Ultimately, you want all the bright red seeds and juice in one bowl and the discards in the other.

Empty the seeds into a food processor and blitz for 3–4 minutes. Empty the contents through a sieve into a bowl, pushing down on the pulp to extract as much juice as possible. Measure this liquid. You should have about 350ml (12fl oz) of juice.

Empty the contents into a small pan with 150ml (5fl oz) of water, the sugar and lime juice. Now taste – you can add a touch more sugar, or more water, at this point, bearing in mind that the jelly will taste less intense when it is set. Sprinkle over the agar flakes or vege-gel and gently heat the liquid to simmering point. Simmer very gently for 5 minutes or until the flakes are fully dissolved. At this stage you can test the jelly by putting a teaspoonful onto a cold plate in the freezer to see if it sets. Pour into the glasses (or you could set it in your leftover lime halves) and set in the fridge for a few hours. Serve straight up or with gently whipped cream or ice cream.

ALTERNATIVE

POMEGRANATE MARGARITA JELLIES

Make the recipe as above but pour in 100ml (3½fl oz) good-quality unaged tequila before heating and up the jelly to 3 tablespoons. Pour into martini glasses to set. Great for after dinner!

MANGO & CHOCOLATE PALETAS

Paletas, which are essentially Mexican lollies made from the many tropical fruits native to the country, are an exceptionally pleasing way to slake one's thirst in such a hot climate. The mango version below is delicious dipped into the Chilli-lime-salt on page 132, while the Mexican chocolate one is made with almond milk and drizzled with white chocolate and chopped almonds, but you could go for condensed milk or double (heavy) cream for a richer finish. A great way to end a party on a hot summer's day.

MAKES 10–12

MANGO DIPPED IN CHILLI-LIME-SALT

2 small ripe mangoes (220g/8oz)

zest and juice of 1 lime (40ml/1½fl oz)

2–3 tbsp light agave nectar

Chilli-lime-salt, to serve (page 132)

Skin and stone the mangoes and add the flesh (and as much juice as you can) into a blender. Add the lime zest and juice and agave with 300ml (10½fl oz) water and blend to combine.

Taste the mixture and add more agave if needed, remembering to sweeten more than you think necessary, as much of the sweetness disappears once the lollies are frozen. Pour into lolly moulds and freeze for at least 8 hours. Serve dipped into the chilli-lime-salt.

MEXICAN CHOCOLATE

400ml (14fl oz) almond or whole milk

few pinches of ground cinnamon

55g (2oz) dark (bittersweet) chocolate, chopped

55g (2oz) milk chocolate, chopped

1–2 tbsp golden syrup

90g (3oz) white chocolate

50g (2oz) almonds (flaked/slivered)

Add the milk to a heavy-bottomed saucepan and warm over a low heat with the cinnamon and golden syrup. Take the milk off the heat and stir through the chocolate until completely melted. Leave to cool and then pour into lolly moulds. Freeze for at least 8 hours.

To decorate, melt the white chocolate and toast the almonds. Drizzle the paletas with the white chocolate and sprinkle with the almonds.

COCKTAILS, SHRUBS & MARGARITAS

My love affair with tequila may never have got off the ground had it not been for that trip around Mexico at eighteen, which led to the discovery that tequila, crazily delicious and worlds away from the cheap stuff we got at home, was much revered in Mexico and served in its coolest bars and nightspots. It was the beginning of a lifelong love for all agave spirits, mezcal firmly included with all its whisky-like smoky notes. Of course, I was already receptive to the idea of a great drink. My paternal grandmother was something of a mover and shaker. Her love for cocktails knew no bounds and I remember many parties in Wales with drinks gayly mixed in her Asprey's cocktail shaker.

I am in drinks for quality not quantity. I want to revel in their sophistication and glamour, be seduced by their taste and hopefully never be *too* won over by their alluring appeal. That said, the explosion of soft cocktails, shrubs and other fermented, gut-friendly low or no-alcohol drinks has been fascinating to see over the last few years. I love a great vinegar stirred into a sparkling mix of fizzy water, good juice, bitters and citrus. Muddle me some fresh herbs and add a great mixer and I am happy without the stronger stuff.

So, sift your way through this troupe of cocktails, tepaches and shrubs, pulling out the ones that suit your mood and the occasion. There is something in here for everyone, and I hope they will bring a jaunty flair to your parties. Happy shaking xxx.

DRINKING VINEGARS & FERMENTED FRUIT SHRUBS

As the years gallop on, I find myself approaching life more gently; it is still intense and insanely busy, but these days I try to give myself a fighting chance. I am increasingly seduced by the lure of a brilliant read and an early night.

This is where these shrubs, or drinking vinegars, fit in. Often I don't feel like a drink and the accompanying foggy head. I want to stay focused and alert and, knowing more about the importance of good gut health, it is a breath of fresh air to know that one can sip a mouthwatering, thirst-quenching vinegar cocktail that does the world of good.

These shrubs are that and more. Top them with sparkling water for a frisson of excitement; serve them neat over ice; add them to salad dressings or use as mixers should you decide, in fact, that a stiff drink is what you needed after all. They are the business. Or sick, as my eldest would say.

Shrubs are best made with an organic live vinegar – it is incredible how many delicious apple cider vinegars are out there for starters. Equally, do experiment with wine vinegars. Making a shrub is also a genius way to save a few handfuls of fruit that you fear may end up looking forlorn at the back of the fridge. Simply crush them, mix and store.

BASE RECIPE

This base recipe is a guide. The general rule of thumb is to use equal parts sugar and vinegar but I find this a little too sweet for my taste. Experiment with the below, halving the recipe if you feel more comfortable, and see how you go. In general, the more sugar you use, the longer it will preserve, but I find mine disappear long before there is any chance of them going off. Using pure caster sugar gives the cleanest taste, but I like to mix this up with honey, agave or unrefined sugar. Choose the most seasonal fruits you can get your hands on and have fun!

MAKES A LARGE BOTTLE (VO)

500g (1lb 2oz) fruit
20–50g (¾–2oz) fresh herbs/secondary flavour
350g (12oz) sugar (I suggest 200g (7oz) caster (superfine) and 150g (5oz) Demerara or panela sugar)
500ml (17fl oz) apple cider vinegar

Add the fruit, herbs and sugar to a large Kilner jar. Muddle with a rolling pin until the fruit is crushed and everything is well mixed. Close the container and leave for 3–4 days at room temperature.

Add the vinegar, shake the container to combine, and then refrigerate for 1–2 weeks. Strain the liquid through a sieve, or through a muslin for a clearer cordial.

Sterilise the jar/bottle you would like to store the finished cordial in. Once bottled, the vinegar will last for 6 months if refrigerated.

GREAT FLAVOUR COMBOS

Rhubarb & ginger (slice the rhubarb into 1cm/½ inch thick rounds, grate the ginger)	Pineapple & mint
	Strawberry & lemon verbena/Thai basil
Raspberry & hibiscus	Watermelon, chilli & lime
Blackberry & bay	

A PAIR OF AGUA FRESCAS

Heretical as it may sound, I do not rush to make a tropical fruit agua fresca when I am at home in the UK. Sure, when I am basking in the intense, baking heat of Mexico, in a puddle of humidity, a refreshing agua is often a lifesaver, but in the temperate climate of Blighty, the idea of blitzing often-expensive exotic fruit with sugar and water just doesn't quite make sense to me. I would rather eat a watermelon in a salad or devour a pineapple in a salsa. However, switch that exotic fruit for something more home-grown, or with a lovely floral note, and I start getting excited. An agua is just that bit more interesting than a glass of water and a nifty way to garner the fresh notes of a cucumber or to enjoy the tart, cranberry-like taste of a hibiscus flower, both of which are packed with vitamin C. Go easy on the sugar, top with sparkling water if you fancy some fizz, and then you are in business. Agua me up, baby!

CUCUMBER AGUA FRESCA

There is little more refreshing than cucumber-scented water. I often just speed-peel long lengths into a jug of iced water with a handful of fresh mint. Eminently cooling. This is not much more work than that and great for a party.

MAKES 1 LITRE (1 QUART) (VO)

300g (10½oz) cucumber

60ml (2fl oz) lime juice

50g (2oz) sugar, or more to taste

big handful of mint leaves

ice, to serve

mint sprigs and lime wheels, to garnish

Put all the ingredients, plus 400ml (14fl oz) water, in a blender and blitz until smooth. Pass through a sieve. Pour in more water to taste – another 400ml (14fl oz) should do it. Then serve over ice with the mint sprigs and lime wheels.

COOK'S NOTE If you like the idea of a hibiscus margarita, just shake a reduced hibiscus syrup with triple sec or Cointreau, the juice of a lime and plenty of tequila.

HIBISCUS AGUA FRESCA

Known as *flor de Jamaica* in Mexico, hibiscus flowers make a delicious, ruby-coloured drink that lies somewhere between Ribena and cranberry juice in taste. They are available from most Middle Eastern grocers or specialist Mexican suppliers. The flowers are good in salsas, ketchups and dressings.

MAKES 2 LITRES (2 QUARTS) (VO)

50g (2oz) dried hibiscus flowers

200g (7oz) caster (superfine) sugar

juice of 3 limes

ice, to serve

sparkling water (optional)

Put the hibiscus flowers, sugar and 2 litres (2 quarts) of water in a large pan and bring to the boil. Simmer briskly for about 30 minutes to extract maximum flavour from the hibiscus flowers. Strain the flowers through a sieve. You can use the strained flowers to decorate the glasses or add a little caster sugar and red wine vinegar to them and put them in salads or empanadas (page 99).

Add the lime juice to the cordial and taste. You may want to add a little more sugar. Cool and serve over ice, perhaps with a little sparkling water to lighten up the flavour.

TEPACHE & PINEAPPLE VINEGAR

Tepache is a bewitching fermented drink from Mexico that uses up all the leftover peel and core from their especially sweet and sharp pineapples (Mexican pineapples are honestly the most delicious you will ever try). Since we import pineapples from the other side of the world, it seems fitting to have a recipe that uses up every last bit of them. And in the words of food writer Mark Diacono, who inspired me to give this a go, 'Expect a sweet, heady aromatic juice that sends cocktail ideas spinning around your mind'. Genius. This is, as you might expect, sensational with a dram of good tequila added for good measure.

FILLS A KILNER JAR (VO)

peel and core from a large, ripe pineapple

150g (5oz) unrefined sugar

large thumb of ginger, sliced

1 red chilli, sliced

4 cloves

2 star anise

TO SERVE

sparkling water

lime juice

tequila (optional)

Lightly wash the pineapple under a little running water – you want to get rid of any dust and dirt (and possible fruit fly) but not scrub it so clean that you lose the good microbes. Top and tail the pineapple and discard these pieces. Cut away the peel, leaving a generous layer of fruit still attached. How much you leave to eat and how much you give to your tepache is a balance that only you can decide, but let's just say that an aromatic tepache cannot be made by peel alone.

Cut the pineapple flesh into quarters and remove the core. Save the fruit for the Caribbean Pineapple Ceviche on page 138 or the Pineapple Tarte Tatin on page 184 or just for eating, perhaps sprinkled with the Chilli-lime-salt on page 132.

Now, empty the sugar into a large 1.5–2 litre (1½–2 quart) Kilner jar and pour 100ml (3½fl oz) boiling water over it. Stir to dissolve and then wedge in the pineapple cores and all the fleshy pieces of skin. Add the ginger, chilli and spices, then top up with water, leaving a few inches of space at the top of the jar. Cover with a piece of muslin and leave out on the counter for 3–4 days, skimming off any white foam on the last day.

Strain the tepache through a sieve into a bottle. You can get a second fermentation from the fruit left behind. Just add more sugar and boiling water, and top with cold. The bottle can be left out to ferment for a few more days, which will make the drink less sweet, and a little tarter. It is delicious topped with sparkling water and a squeeze of lime.

COOK'S NOTE If you want to go one step further, ferment for a few weeks instead of a few days and you will be rewarded with a pineapple vinegar on your windowsill like a true Mexican mama.

OLD FASHIONED

Everything about this cocktail is considered: the liquor stirred slowly through crystal-cold ice, the sultry, smoky tones of the ingredients and the crescendo of warmth it creates as it slips down your throat and travels on. It is an after-dinner drink for when, satiated from the food, you are ready for the evening to take a different turn. This will put fire in your belly, a glint in your eye and a spring in your step.

MAKES A GLASS

| 7.5ml (¼fl oz) agave syrup |
| few dashes of Angostura bitters (or try orange or chocolate bitters for fun) |
| 50ml (2fl oz) añejo tequila |
| ribbon of pink grapefruit peel |
| ribbon of orange peel |
| ice, to serve |

Fill a tumbler with ice. Pour over the agave, bitters and tequila and stir until the glass feels cold. Add more ice to the top.

Cut away a ribbon each of grapefruit and orange peel. Squeeze the oils in the skin over the cocktail, twist the ribbons and drop into the tumbler. Serve to your favourite after-dinner guest or to yourself as you settle down to watching *Casablanca* for the fiftieth time or a great French arthouse movie or *True Romance* on repeat.

BLACK RUSSIAN

It seems like a delicious quirk of fate that the cocktail that will go down in our family's history contains a coffee liqueur that is made in one of my favourite states in Mexico, Veracruz. My glamorous grandmother, originally from Tennessee, was known for her love of cocktails – in fact Humphrey Bogart once bought her one in a New York cocktail bar apparently because he so admired her hat. Cut to Wales many years later, where my grandmother then lived. Some good friends of ours knew how to throw a mean party, and it was Black Russians that they would hand out after dinner. On one infamous night, Granny Jean had so many Black Russians that she started revealing various family secrets that had never before been aired. The party lasted well into the small hours, which may explain why no clear detail of my grandmother's tales could ever be remembered. Perhaps it was the Black Russians.

FOR 1 OR 2, DEPENDING ON WHO'S LOOKING

| 50ml (2fl oz) mezcal, or vodka if you prefer the classic |
| 25ml (1fl oz) Kahlúa |
| dash of orange bitters |
| ice, to serve |

Pour the mezcal, Kahlúa and bitters into a mixing glass over ice. Stir until well chilled, then strain into a tumbler filled with fresh ice.

If you prefer something creamy, shake in a few tablespoons of single (light) cream for a white Russian.

PINK GRAPEFRUIT MEZCAL SOUR

This recipe was made for me by Oliver Pergl, an inspired barman and agave enthusiast who could tell you a thing or two about agave spirits. His own spirit of generosity knows no bounds, nor does his passion for tequila and mezcal. We were talking about sours, my favourite type of cocktail, so he made me this one. It really is delicious. If you are vegan, use aquafaba to create the classic sour 'foam'. And if you don't have yellow chartreuse lurking in your drinks cupboard, just leave it out and replace with mezcal (you will just need to adjust the sweetness).

MAKES 1

35ml (1fl oz) mezcal

15ml (½fl oz) yellow chartreuse

juice of 1 lime

1 egg white or 1 tsp aquafaba (chickpea water)

25ml (1fl oz) pink grapefruit juice

3 dashes of grapefruit bitters

12.5ml (½fl oz) agave syrup

ice, to serve

ribbon of pink grapefruit peel, to garnish

Shake all the ingredients hard over ice and strain into an ice-filled glass.

Garnish with a piece of grapefruit peel, squeezing it over the surface of the drink to spray it with the oils in the grapefruit skin.

MY SMOKY MARTINIS

A smoky, sultry, spicy drink inspired by a cocktail I once had in a ranch in the Yucatán. A drink to set the mood of an evening.

MAKES 1

50ml (1¾fl oz) mezcal

15ml (½fl oz) lime juice

10ml (¼fl oz) fresh orange juice

15ml (½fl oz) habanero syrup

1 egg white or 1 tsp aquafaba (chickpea water)

cayenne pepper

ice, to serve

FOR THE SYRUP

1 dried habanero chilli (or try using a fresh Scotch bonnet), roughly chopped

200ml (7fl oz) agave syrup

TO GARNISH

small pinch of cayenne pepper

slice of orange

To make the syrup, mix the habanero, agave and 100ml (3½fl oz) water together and bring to a gentle boil. Simmer gently for 3–4 minutes, tasting the syrup as it simmers and taking it off the heat once it has reached the heat level you are comfortable with. Allow to cool, strain and then pour into a sterilised bottle.

Shake all the cocktail ingredients hard in a shaker for 5 seconds, then fill with ice and shake on ice for around 10 seconds. Strain into an ice-filled glass and garnish with a small pinch of cayenne pepper and a slice of orange.

SANGRITA & VERDITA

In Mexico a glass of tequila sipped before lunch or dinner is traditionally accompanied by a small glass of sangrita. Sangrita is a vividly spicy Virgin Mary-style tomato juice seasoned with Tabasco and the bright citrus juices of orange, lime and pomegranate. Recently, it has also become fashionable to pair tequila with a Verdita as well – a refreshing, chilli and herb-spiked bright green pineapple juice – although I love to make this with a more local cloudy apple juice. Both do a great job of whetting the appetite at the beginning of a feast, so try the recipes here and work out your favourite. Delicious on their own, they can also double up as a mixer for a longer, tequila-based cocktail.

SANGRITA

MAKES 4 (VO)

300ml (10½fl oz) good-quality tomato juice

juice of 1 orange

juice of 1–2 limes

20ml (¾fl oz) grenadine or 30ml (1fl oz) fresh pomegranate juice

½ tsp Tabasco

1 tbsp Worcestershire sauce

1 tsp sea salt

freshly ground black pepper

50ml red wine (optional)

TO SERVE

ice

lime wedges

dusting of chilli powder (page 17)

tequila (optional)

Shake the ingredients over ice and pour into small shot glasses or a tumbler filed with ice, if you love a Virgin Mary. Add a double shot of tequila to the tumbler to make a Bloody Maria.

VERDITA

MAKES 4 (VO)

300ml (10½fl oz) cloudy apple or pineapple juice

1 celery stick

1 jalapeño chilli, de-stalked

small bunch of coriander (cilantro)

small bunch of mint

30ml (1fl oz) lime juice

ice, to serve

Blitz the ingredients in a blender and pour through a strainer. Pour into a jug filled with ice and serve with glasses of tequila.

THE MARGARITAS

In my book there is always room for a margarita. It is the best cocktail at a party. Tequila is made from agaves that bask for years in Mexican sunshine – that sunshine seeps into the agave which is distilled into the happiest of drinks; it coaxes you, urges you to dance as if you have had a pair of magic red slippers slipped onto your feet. Serve them before or after dinner for a great night.

TOMMI'S CLASSIC MARGARITA

In this version of the classic, agave syrup is used to sweeten the cocktail instead of triple sec. The result is pure and refreshing: with vitamin C from the fresh lime, low-GI sugars from the agave syrup and a wholly uplifting taste.

MAKES 2

70ml (2½fl oz) blanco tequila (we use El Tesoro)

50ml (1¾fl oz) lime juice

30ml (1fl oz) agave syrup

wedge of lime

Shake all the ingredients over ice and pour into a tumbler loaded with ice, or a martini glass if you prefer it straight up. Garnish with a wedge of lime and a salt rim, if desired.

TAMARIND MARGARITA

Wahaca had a tamarind margarita for years simply to keep me happy. Tamarind is sold in sweet form in Mexico, covered in a chilli-sugar-salt and wrapped in brightly coloured wrappers. It is sensational in this margarita.

MAKES 2

70ml (2½fl oz) tamarind paste (from 70g/2½oz peeled tamarind) (page 245)

70ml (2½fl oz) tequila

30ml (1fl oz) triple sec

ice, to serve

wedge of lime

Shake all the ingredients over ice and pour into a tumbler. Garnish with a wedge of lime and a chilli-sugar-salt rim.

THE RIM

Always consider the salt rim, invented to mellow the bitter notes of a margarita and get the taste buds working. Rub the top few millimetres of the outside edge of the glass with a cut wedge of lemon, lime or orange. Roll the glass lightly in a small plate filled with any of the below, using an angle of around 45 degrees.

CHILLI-SUGAR-SALT

See page 132 for recipe. Experiment with different chilli powders and add lime zest depending on the cocktail.

HIBISCUS-SUGAR

Blitz 10g (¼oz) dried hibiscus flowers in a spice grinder to a fine powder. Sift to discard any larger pieces of the plant. Stir into 40g (1½oz) caster (superfine) sugar.

SHISO-SUGAR-SALT

A bit poncy, but I have been growing a pot of shiso indoors and the leaves are amazing in cocktails. Finely chop a small handful of dried shiso leaves and stir into 15g (½oz) sea salt and 10g (¼oz) sugar and the zest of 1 orange. Also good with ground hoja santa leaves (page 12) or dried mint leaves.

THE FROZEN MARGARITAS

STRAWBERRY, BALSAMIC AND TARRAGON

A glorious celebration of the exuberance that summer fruits bring with a frisson of sophistication from the tarragon and vinegar.

MAKES 2

140g (5oz) ripe strawberries

small handful of tarragon leaves, about 10g (¼oz)

40ml (1½fl oz) tequila

30ml (1fl oz) Cointreau

25ml (1fl oz) lime juice

1 tsp balsamic vinegar (I love the Pedro Ximénez balsamic)

3 handfuls of ice

Blitz everything in a blender and serve in two frozen martini glasses. I really like a hibiscus-sugar rim here (page 220), preferably with a shake of pul biber chillies.

ELDERFLOWER & BANANA

It might sound like a cocktail for kindergarten, but this is a stunning subtle drink for a hot summer's evening. Stash peeled bananas in the freezer when they are threatening to go over – they are perfect for throwing into the blender.

MAKES 2

150g (5oz) frozen banana

3 handfuls of ice

85ml (3fl oz) 100% agave unaged (blanco) tequila

25ml (1fl oz) triple sec

30ml (1fl oz) elderflower cordial

30ml (1fl oz) lime juice

Blitz the bananas and ice together. Pour in the rest of the ingredients and blitz until smooth. Pour into frozen martini glasses. These are great with a lime zest-sugar rim (page 220).

MANGO SLUSH PUPPY

In late April and early May, the first wave of mangoes starts to arrive in the UK from overseas. Initially it is the larger Alphonso mangoes that appear and cause the excitement, then in early June it is the time of the honey mangoes from India and Pakistan. They are packed five or six to the box, nestled in and protected by bright yellow tissue paper with colourful strands of sparkly tinsel cheerfully hanging from the boxes. Mango heaven.

MAKES 3

3 ripe honey mangoes or 2 Alphonso

50ml (1¾fl oz) triple sec

70ml (2½fl oz) tequila

30ml (1fl oz) lime juice

100g (3½oz) ice

Blend the flesh of the mangoes, the triple sec, tequila and lime juice with the ice until completely smooth. Pour into glasses, with the rims dusted in Chilli-sugar-salt (page 220), preferably using dried habanero chilli, in small amounts!

SALSAS, CHILLI OILS & MAYOS

When I first travelled to Mexico, I was under the impression that chillies were red or green and either hot or blistering. What I found instead was a cuisine that used the many different flavours of the different varieties. Dried chillies are piled up in big sacks in the markets with a dizzying collection of exotic names, shapes and sizes; fresh ones are in the vegetable sections in small, tempting heaps. The dried chillies I tried were smoky, earthy, sweet, spicy and used for moles, (complex sauces of ground nuts, spices and chillies, marinades and braises), while the fresh chillies add a sprinkling of top note heat to food rather like black pepper does.

With a small range of chillies, you can experiment with this collection of salsas and sauces to add these layers of exciting flavour and depth to your food. Try a simple home-made mayo seasoned with a smoky chipotle or a charred jalapeño; a chilli-tomato jam; a few chilli oils that we eat with everything or salsa negra, with its smoky, sweet, slow heat. Grab handfuls of herbs and whizz them together to make vibrant, fresh salsas; grill spring onions (scallions) for Asian-influenced relishes; toss slender sliced red onions in fresh citrus juices to add colour and vim to your dishes.

I hope that you will get stuck into this chapter more than any other in the book and fall in love with the intoxicating tastes that chillies weave into your food. I hope you have fun!

SALSAS

FRESH TOMATO PICO

This salsa, the classic *pico de gallo*, is fresh, citrussy and delicious, especially when made with great tomatoes. Not only does it look good sprinkled over dishes, glistening with the oil and lime, but it adds sparkling acidity to anything you ladle it on. Make it all summer when tomatoes are blooming, or with those wonderful winter varieties, keeping them outside the fridge to maintain their sweet, delicate flavour.

MAKES A LARGE BOWL (VO)

6 very ripe plum or cherry tomatoes

small handful of coriander (cilantro)

1 small red onion, very finely diced

1–2 green chillies, preferably jalapeños, very finely chopped

1 tbsp extra-virgin olive oil

juice of 1–2 limes

1 tsp sea salt

1 tsp soft brown sugar

salt and pepper

Cut the tomatoes into quarters and scoop out the watery insides (you can keep them and use them in a vinaigrette or in a soup). Dice the flesh.

Roughly chop the coriander leaves and finely chop the stalks and stir into the tomatoes with the onion, chillies, oil, half the lime juice, the salt and sugar. Check the flavour and add more salt, pepper or lime juice if you think the salsa needs it. Leave to marinate for at least 20 minutes before you are ready to eat.

This is delicious with the Baked Feta and Pickled Chilli Nachos on page 66, as a light salad to go with Blistered Green Bean Tacos (page 88) and sprinkled over roast vegetables (page 164).

SALSA NEGRA

This concentrated chilli paste comes from Veracruz, home of the jalapeño chilli, which when smoked and dried becomes a chipotle. It is smoky and spicy with sweet undertones, transforming the Fideus on page 116 and the Sweetcorn Nuggets on page 70. Try it as a garnish on any soup with a dollop of crème fraîche or Homemade Crema (page 242).

MAKES 260G (9OZ)

180ml (6fl oz) rapeseed (canola) or groundnut oil

15g (½oz) árbol chillies, de-stemmed and de-seeded

25g (1oz) chipotle chillies, de-stemmed and de-seeded and cut into pieces

10 black garlic cloves, chopped

10 fresh garlic cloves, chopped

1 tbsp red wine vinegar

1 tbsp light brown sugar

½ tsp cumin seeds

1 tsp salt

In a large saucepan, combine the oil and the chillies and bring to a simmer over a medium–low heat, stirring frequently, until fragrant and the chillies are slightly browning in spots, about 5–7 minutes.

Stir in both garlics, the vinegar, sugar, cumin and salt and take off the heat after 2 minutes. Allow to cool, then transfer the mixture to a blender and blitz until you have a smooth paste. Taste and adjust the seasoning for a balance of sweet, savoury and spicy. It will last for weeks in the fridge.

COOK'S NOTE Bear in mind that salsas always taste hotter when you taste them on their own. Once they are layered onto food, much of their heat is sucked away by the carbohydrates, so be bold and brave when adding chillies and see pages 14 and 17 for more info on the different varieties.

ROAST CHIPOTLE SALSA

A simple, smoky, rounded salsa that you can pull together with very little effort to dress tacos, quesadillas and nachos. The dried chillies, which could be cascabel or árbol, will give the salsa depth of flavour (and more heat in the case of the árbol), but adding them is an entirely personal preference. You can simply dry-roast a few fresh jalapeños or standard red bullet chillies in the pan instead. When making salsa, the world is your oyster: experimenting with the different flavour profiles that fresh and dried chillies bring is all part of the fun.

MAKES A SMALL BOWL (VO)

5 ripe plum tomatoes

2 garlic cloves, unpeeled

1 onion, peeled and cut into 6–8 wedges

few dried chillies (optional)

½ tsp sea salt

1 tbsp Chipotles en Adobo (page 234), or more to taste

small handful of coriander (cilantro)

½ tsp brown sugar

juice of ½ lime

splash of vinegar (optional)

salt and pepper

Heat your oldest frying pan (skillet) over a high heat. You do not want to use your best pan here! Add the whole tomatoes, garlic and onion wedges and dry-roast, turning every few minutes, until they are blackened, blistered and soft (page 244). The tomatoes and onions will take 10–15 minutes, while the garlic takes less time, about 6–7 minutes. Towards the end, toast the dried chillies, if using, for 30–40 seconds a side until smelling nutty. Remove and finely chop.

When the garlic is cooked, slip the cloves from their skins and put in a pestle and mortar with the sea salt, the chipotle and the dried chillies. Finely chop the coriander stalks and add these too. Work into a paste and then work in the onion, chopping it up a bit with a pair of scissors. Finally, add the tomatoes, mashing them in.

Stir in the sugar, lime juice and vinegar, plus the roughly chopped coriander leaves. Taste and adjust the seasoning, adding more salt or lime and vinegar, to taste.

Alternatively, you can blitz the salsa in a food processor. The texture will be different but when you are in a rush, it saves time.

SMOKY HIBISCUS SALSA

A sweet, smoky ketchup, this makes a brilliant dip for the Sweet Potato Chunks on page 76.

FILLS A LARGE JAM JAR (vo)

40ml (1½fl oz) olive oil

1 onion, finely chopped

2 garlic cloves, chopped

5g (⅛oz) dried hibiscus flowers or 1 tbsp pomegranate molasses

1 tbsp brown sugar, or more to taste

1 x 400g (14oz) tin of plum tomatoes, drained and rinsed

2–4 tsp Chipotles en Adobo (page 234) or 1 tsp sweet paprika

salt and pepper

Heat a saucepan over a medium–high heat and when hot, add the oil. Add the onion and garlic and cook gently for 10–15 minutes until the onion is soft and sweet.

Meanwhile, blitz the hibiscus flowers in a spice grinder to get a fine powder. Add to the onion and season with salt, pepper and the sugar. When the onion is soft, add the rest of the ingredients, squishing the tomatoes through your hands as you do or breaking up with a wooden spoon.

Add 100ml (3½fl oz) water and bring to the boil. Simmer for 30 minutes, then whizz with a stick blender until you have a smooth, spoonable purée, adding a splash more water if needed. Check the seasoning and serve warm or at room temperature.

SWEET CASCABEL & TOMATILLO SALSA

This fruity, rounded, tomatillo-based salsa is seriously good. Without the árbol chillies adding fire it is fairly mild, so it can be spooned onto food with relish; with the árbol chillies there is a wonderful slow build of heat that fills the mouth and contrasts with the sweet, fruity notes of the cascabel and ancho. Particularly good over any type of toast you may want for brunch or try over sautéed greens on ricotta toast or with a fried egg.

MAKES A SMALL BOWL (vo)

50g (2oz) cascabel chillies

2 ancho chillies (20g/¾oz)

2 tbsp olive or vegetable oil

½ red onion, finely diced

3 garlic cloves, crushed

1 tsp cumin seeds

1–2 árbol chillies (optional)

300g (10oz) fresh or tinned tomatillos or tomatillo salsa

150g (5oz) large tomatoes, roughly chopped

1 tsp brown sugar

salt and pepper

Tear open the cascabel and ancho chillies, removing their stems and seeds. Tear, snip or blitz into smaller pieces.

Heat a saucepan over a medium heat with the oil and add the onion and garlic. Sweat in the oil for 5 minutes, then add the chillies and cumin and sweat for a further 5 minutes until smelling fragrant. Add the árbol chillies, if using, at this stage, de-stemmed and roughly chopped. Season with 1 teaspoon of salt and lots of black pepper and empty in the tomatillos, tomatoes and sugar with 350ml (12fl oz) water.

Bring up to heat and simmer gently for 20–25 minutes, then purée with a blender or in a food processor. Taste and adjust the seasoning with more salt, vinegar or fresh lemon juice.

TOMATILLO SALSA

AKA SALSA VERDE

Tomatillos, related to the cape gooseberry, are wonderfully tart and citrussy. This fresh salsa takes moments to make and adds acidity and vibrancy to many different Mexican dishes. Try it tossed with green vegetables and cream for a filling for tamales (page 101) or mix with crema (vegan or otherwise) for a sensationally citrussy topping for an enchilada (page 163); add avocado to make tomatillo guac (see note) or useon nachos, drizzled over tacos or paired with the Achiote-grilled Halloumi on page 141.

MAKES A SMALL BOWL (VO)

80g (3oz) green apple

500g (1lb 2oz) fresh or tinned tomatillos

½ white onion

small bunch of coriander (cilantro), roughly chopped

1–2 jalapeño chillies, roughly chopped

1 garlic clove, roughly chopped

small knob of ginger, finely grated

juice of ½ lime

½ tsp salt

Peel the apple. If you are using fresh tomatillos, peel away the husks, wipe with a clean damp cloth and plunge into a pan of boiling water with the onion and once simmering again, blanch for 30 seconds. If you are using tinned tomatillos, drain them.

Put the peeled apple, coriander, chillies, garlic and ginger in a food processor with the tomatillos, blanched or tinned. Blitz to a purée with 100ml (3½fl oz) water, the lime juice and salt. Taste and adjust the heat with more chilli, if you would like, and the seasoning. Set aside in the fridge for the flavours to get to know one another. The salsa will 'set' a little, so you will probably need to stir in a few more tablespoons of water to let it down when you come to eat.

ALTERNATIVE

TOMATILLO-GUACAMOLE

For a slightly creamier version of a tomatillo salsa, try blending 50:50 tomatillo salsa and avocado and then check for seasoning, adding more lime, diced shallot, chilli or coriander (cilantro) to taste.

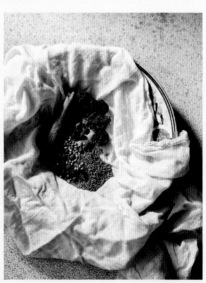

SWEET TOMATO-CHILLI JAM

My husband complains bitterly when we run out of this jam. He dollops it on sausages and lamb chops and scoffs it with cheese. It is a great way to preserve tomatoes in the high summer when they are bursting with sweetness. Haggle with stall holders at the end of market days to buy them cheap. If you haven't got a muslin, you can add the spices straight to the pan, but fish out the cinnamon stick at the end of cooking, even if you leave in the rest. This jam will last for 3 months in sterilised jars and is delicious with the Baked Feta on page 66 or the Cheddar Cheese and Pickled Jalapeño scones on page 81.

MAKES 2–3 JAM JARS (VO)

- 1.5kg (3lb 5oz) tomatoes
- 3 tbsp olive or rapeseed (canola) oil
- 2 large red onions, chopped
- 25g (1oz) ginger, peeled and chopped
- 5 garlic cloves, chopped
- 2 tsp cumin seeds
- 2 tbsp coriander seeds
- 2 star anise
- 1 or 2 fresh Scotch bonnet chillies, roughly chopped, or 2 dried habaneros
- 1 cinnamon stick
- 150ml (5fl oz) good-quality cider vinegar
- 175g (6oz) soft brown sugar
- 175g (6oz) caster (superfine) sugar
- zest and juice of 1–2 limes
- salt

To make the jam, first wash two jam jars in hot soapy water, then place in a 100°C/80°C fan /250°F/gas ½ oven for 20 minutes or so to dry out and sterilise.

Cover the tomatoes with boiling water for 30 seconds. Drain and peel, squeezing the tomato juice from the skins into a bowl with the peeled tomatoes.

Warm the oil in a deep pan over a medium heat and cook the onions, ginger and garlic and a pinch of salt until soft, about 10 minutes.

Wrap all the spices except the cinnamon stick in muslin or a square of J-cloth or add loose.

Add the tomatoes, chillies, 1 tablespoon of salt, the vinegar and sugar and bring to a simmer. Cook, stirring to make sure it's not sticking, for 1–2 hours over a low heat until dark, jammy and thick. Check the seasoning, adding more salt if needed.

Add the lime zest and juice to taste. Cool and then pour into the sterilised jam jars, discarding the muslin bag of spices.

COOK'S NOTES This is a loose jam. If you would prefer a more 'set' version, use jam sugar instead of caster.

CHIPOTLES EN ADOBO
A SMOKED CHILLI PASTE THAT NO COOK SHOULD DO WITHOUT

En adobo means 'in a sauce or marinade'. This smoky, fiery, slightly sweet purée harnesses the intense flavours of chipotle chillies (which are dried jalapeños) and gives them body with the sweet acidity of tomatoes and floral notes from the herbs. It is utterly delicious and can be added to stews, pasta sauces, dressings and mayonnaises. You can buy it in jars, but the home-made version is a hundred times better. When you have made it once, you will wonder how you ever did without it.

MAKES ABOUT 1 LITRE (1 QUART)

200g (7oz) chipotle chillies (about 65)

1 large Spanish onion, roughly chopped

1 head of garlic, cloves roughly chopped

3 tbsp oregano leaves or a few good pinches of dried oregano

1–2 tbsp thyme leaves

2 fresh bay leaves

2 tsp allspice

2 tsp cumin seeds, crushed

4 tbsp olive oil

175ml (6fl oz) good-quality cider vinegar

175ml (6fl oz) good-quality balsamic vinegar

3 tbsp tomato purée (paste)

150–200g (5–7oz) Demerara sugar, to taste

2 tbsp sea salt

Wash the chipotles in cold water and drain. Snip off the stalk end of each chilli with scissors, which will allow the water to penetrate their tough skins. Put in a medium saucepan, cover with water and simmer for about 40 minutes until completely soft. When the chillies are soft, rinse off any seeds.

Put the onion, garlic, herbs, allspice and cumin into a blender with 200ml (7fl oz) of water and half the chillies. Purée to a smooth paste.

Heat the olive oil in a large, heavy-bottomed saucepan until it is smoking hot. Add the chilli paste and fry for about 3 minutes, stirring continuously with a spatula to prevent it catching and burning.

Add the vinegars, tomato purée, sugar, salt and another 200ml (7fl oz) water and cook for 5 more minutes before adding the rest of the chillies. Cook for another 5 minutes, then purée the mixture before continuing to cook for 10 minutes over a low heat, stirring every so often to stop the sauce from burning. Taste to check the seasoning, adding more salt or sugar if needed. If you like, you can whizz the whole lot again with a stick blender to a rough paste or store as is in clean, sterilised jam or Kilner jars. Like ketchup, I store this in the fridge for many months – at least 3–6!

COOK'S NOTE This recipe makes a generous amount so you can halve it, but you will find yourself using it a lot. Making lots is very little extra work and jars of it make THE most fantastic present.

RELISHES

QUICK CORIANDER CHIMICHURRI SALSA

A very fast, very easy Mexican-inspired chimichurri or a coriander oil, you will want to drizzle it over everything.

MAKES A SMALL BOWL (vo)

1 garlic clove, very finely chopped

½ tsp cumin seeds

1 tsp hot paprika

1 red chilli, de-seeded and finely chopped

1 tbsp red wine vinegar

100ml (3½fl oz) olive oil

bunch of coriander (cilantro), leaves and stalks chopped

3 handfuls of parsley leaves, chopped

salt and pepper

Whizz up all the ingredients in a food processor or bash together in a pestle and mortar for a rougher texture.

Stored in an airtight container in the fridge, this will keep for 2 weeks, though ensure it is under oil.

CHARRED ONION & CORIANDER EVERYDAY RELISH

The flavours in this citrussy chopped salsa are so versatile that it goes with almost anything. Ladle it over nachos, eat it with fritters, spoon it over eggs. I love chopping so I do this by hand – it gives the salsa great texture – but by all means, whizz in a blender.

MAKES A LARGE BOWL (vo)

2 garlic cloves

1 tsp sea salt

60g (2oz) spring onions (scallions), trimmed and outer skins discarded

1–2 hot green chillies, finely chopped

3 handfuls of coriander (cilantro), stalks and leaves, finely chopped

1 large handful of mint leaves, finely chopped

1 tsp dried oregano

60ml (2fl oz) lime juice (from 1–2 limes)

100ml (3½fl oz) olive oil

1 tbsp cider vinegar

1 tsp unrefined caster (superfine) sugar

Bash the garlic cloves once to release their skins, then mash to a purée with the sea salt. Scrape into a medium-size bowl.

Lay the spring onions out on a hot frying pan (skillet) or griddle pan with the chillies and grill on all sides until charred and soft, 3–5 minutes.

Finely chop the spring onions and chillies and add all the onions and half the chillies to the bowl. Add the coriander stalks and leaves and mint to the bowl with the oregano.

Now, stir in the lime juice, olive oil, vinegar and sugar. Taste and add more salt if needed, and the rest of the chilli if you would like, remembering that the heat in salsas is always reduced when you eat them with starchy foods. Serve in lovely salsa pots for people to help themselves.

CHILLI OILS

AJILLO OIL

This oil is named after the guajillo chilli used to give it its attractive rusty colour, and the liberal use of garlic in it (garlic is *ajo* in Spanish), which is cooked slowly until soft, sweet and caramelised. It is a sweet, nutty, rich chilli oil that can be as mild or spicy as you desire. I often make a mild one, with only a few árbol chillies, and it adds wonderful flavour to all food. Toss through the Sweet Potato Chunks on page 76 or rub it over aubergine or courgettes before grilling, or carrots or celeriac before roasting.

MAKES 400ML (14FL OZ) (VO)

60g (2oz) garlic

300ml (10½fl oz) olive or sunflower oil

5–6 guajillo chillies, about 40g (1½oz)

5g árbol chillies, de-stalked

leaves from 6–8 thyme sprigs

zest and juice of ½ lemon

1 tsp sea salt

Bash the garlic cloves once or twice with a heavy object and slip off their skins. Finely chop and add them to a pan with the oil. Put over a medium heat and gently bring up to simmering point. Once the oil is warm and a few bubbles are appearing on the surface, turn the heat right down and very gently poach the garlic in the oil.

Meanwhile, open up the guajillo chillies, de-stemming them and shaking out the seeds. Briefly pulse-blitz them with the árbol chilies in a spice or coffee grinder to get small chilli flakes. Add them to the oil with the thyme.

Cook the chillies and garlic for 20–25 minutes, by which stage the kitchen will be smelling pretty spectacular. Add the lemon zest and juice and the sea salt. Blitz the lot with a stick blender, taste to check the seasoning and store in a sterilised jam jar for 3–6 months.

HABANERO OIL

Fruity, herbaceous and rich-tasting with a fiery backdrop, this is a very simple and pleasing chilli oil to make. Delicious on the Mexican Pizzas (tlayudas) on page 178, I also love it drizzled over salads – try it over chopped raw cauliflower, orange slices and thinly sliced radishes or over the Chargrilled Courgettes on page 144.

MAKES 400ML (14FL OZ)

3 dried habanero chillies, or more to taste

1 tbsp coriander seeds

5 large garlic cloves, unpeeled

1 tsp Mexican oregano (optional)

2 tbsp good-quality cider vinegar

350ml (12fl oz) olive oil

2 tsp sea salt

Soak the habanero chillies in boiling water for 15 minutes.

Now, place a small frying pan (skillet) over a medium heat and toast the coriander seeds and garlic. The coriander will have toasted after 30–40 seconds, or when smelling fragrant; the garlic will soften and turn toasty black in patches after 5–10 minutes.

Transfer them to a small food processor with the habanero chillies, oregano and cider vinegar and blitz. Add a few tablespoons of oil and blitz again until you have a smooth-ish paste, adding more oil to loosen the blades as you need.

Finally, transfer the lot to a small pan, including all the oil and the salt and heat for 10 minutes to allow it to infuse. Store in a sterilised jam jar for 3–6 months.

SALSA MACHA – MY FAVOURITE CHILLI OIL

A macha is a type of chilli oil, blending toasted garlic, peanuts and sesame seeds with the nutty tones of a toasted árbol chilli. It comes from Ensenada, a bustling port on Baja California's coast, with a collection of insanely delicious restaurants and street-food stands. One of these, La Guerrerense, run by Sabina Bandera, makes possibly the best seafood tostadas in Mexico, as vouched for by Salma Hayek. Try adding 20g (¾oz) cascabel chillies for sweet, fruity undertones, or the classic, which has a beautiful dry, searing heat. Drizzle the oil over eggs, noodles, stir-fries and pasta, toss into sautéed greens or add to the Wild Greens Spring Soup on page 114.

ALTERNATIVE MACHA

SWEET CASCABEL MACHA (MEDIUM)

Reduce the árbol chillies to 10g (¼oz). De-stalk and de-seed 30g (1oz) cascabel chillies and cook in the hot oil as right, being careful not to burn them, then proceed as in the main recipe.

CLASSIC PEANUT SALSA MACHA (HOT)

MAKES 500ML (17FL OZ)

30g (1oz) sesame seeds

25g (1oz) árbol chillies

400ml (14fl oz) vegetable oil

5 large garlic cloves, peeled

50g (2oz) peanuts

½ tsp caster (superfine) sugar

1–2 tbsp cider vinegar

1–2 tsp sea salt

Toast the sesame seeds to pale golden in a dry frying pan (skillet). Empty into a food processor and pulse-blitz until the mixture is mostly ground. Now, break open the chillies, shaking out the seeds.

Put half the vegetable oil in a small pan over a medium–low heat (you are looking for approx. 70°C/160°F). Add the garlic cloves and toast for 4–5 minutes until the garlic is pale golden. Remove from the heat with a slotted spoon. Repeat with the peanuts.

Finally, toast the chillies until they gently darken in colour, 30 seconds–1 minute, then remove – you do not want to burn the garlic, nuts or chillies or they will taste bitter. Allow the oil to cool slightly.

Add the chillies and half the nuts to the blender and pulse-blitz. Add the garlic and sugar and pulse a few more times, adding just enough oil to get the motor running. Blitz a few times more to a rough paste. Add the rest of the oil, including the cooking oil, the vinegar and the rest of the nuts and pulse-blitz once more to get a mix of chunky peanuts and some ground.

Taste, adding enough salt so that the chilli oil is tasting rounded and delicious. Empty into a washed and sterilised jam jar, label and store for 3–6 months.

PINK PICKLED ONIONS

These bright citrussy onions are a stunning shade of brilliant pink and they make food come alive. When I have a bowl in the fridge, I find myself scattering them liberally over almost everything. The recipe comes from the Yucatan, where the Spanish conquistadores came and planted great groves of Seville orange trees. The bitter juices of the fruit soon became an integral part of the state's much-feted cuisine in ceviches, salsas and marinades. A mixture of fresh lime and orange started replacing it when Seville oranges became harder to find. Make these mild or spike them with habanero chilli – both will be delicious.

MAKES A BOWL ⓥⓞ

1 red onion, finely sliced

2 tbsp lime juice

2½ tbsp orange juice

½ tsp Mexican oregano (optional)

1 Scotch bonnet or habanero chilli, finely chopped (optional)

If you are short of time, cover the onion in boiling water and soak for 30 seconds, then drain. This will speed up the pickling process. Otherwise, just cover the onion with the citrus juices, scrunching it into the citrus with your hands for 20–30 seconds.

Stir in the oregano and the chilli, if using, and refrigerate, covered, for at least 30 minutes to allow the onion to macerate in the juices. Serve on stews, salads, with fritters and street food for a delicate, crunchy, sparkle of acidity.

BURNT SPRING ONION RELISH

Chicago, also known as 'little Mexico' because of its thriving Mexican community, is a city that knows how to eat well. Packed with incredibly exciting and innovative restaurants, the food is characterised by the melting pot of cultures and people that make up the city. It was on a recce trip there with some of the Wahaca team that we first discovered the joy of Mexican/Korean fusion, a daring umami-rich mash-up of sweet, smoky, spicy and sour tastes. This relish is inspired by that trip.

MAKES A SMALL BOWL

large bunch of spring onions (scallions) (about 200g/7oz)

1½ tbsp mild olive or rapeseed (canola) oil

1 tbsp sesame oil

½ garlic clove, finely chopped

½ tsp grated ginger

juice of ½ lime

1½ tsp soy sauce

1 tsp sherry vinegar

Put a griddle pan over a high heat. Rub the spring onions in ½ tablespoon of the oil and once the griddle is hot, grill the spring onions for 5–6 minutes until charred all over and tender in the middle. Transfer to a board to cool, then chop finely and toss in a bowl with the remaining relish ingredients.

Ladle onto the Crispy Tofu Tacos on page 90 or they are also great with the Sweetcorn Nuggets on page 70.

ALTERNATIVE

QUICK CUCUMBER PICKLE

This quick pickle is another favourite way to add crunch and inject a burst of sweet acidity. Finely slice a cucumber and toss with 1 peeled and finely sliced shallot, ½ teaspoon of fine sea salt, 2 teaspoons of caster (superfine) sugar and 3 tablespoons good-quality cider vinegar. Add a finely chopped red chilli if you want a little heat. Cover and chill before serving.

THREE WONDERFUL HOME-MADE MAYONNAISES

I can think of little in life that isn't improved by a touch of mayonnaise. When it comes to Mexican food, it can be a game deciding what type to make with so many chillies to choose from. I start with an aioli base, from there, it is about picking the chilli according to what flavour variation you are looking for. The below take 10 minutes to make from start to finish.

BASE AIOLI

Use this as your starting point, a good foil for adding the different ingredients below. If in doubt, use fewer chillies to start with – you can always add more to taste later, bearing in mind that once you add the mayo to food, much of the chilli heat will be sucked away.

MAKES A SMALL BOWL

2 egg yolks

2 garlic cloves, crushed with ½ tsp salt

½ tsp Dijon mustard

2 tsp white wine vinegar

150ml (5fl oz) sunflower or groundnut (peanut) oil

150ml (5fl oz) extra-virgin olive oil

Whizz the yolks, garlic, salt and mustard together in a small food processor with whichever of the chillies you are using below. This will make your starting paste, which you will emulsify with the oil.

If whisking by hand, make a dish-towel cradle for a medium-size bowl to stop it spinning around. Transfer the egg and chilli purée to the bowl and slowly drizzle in the oil, drop by drop, whisking or beating continuously with a whisk or wooden spoon. Keep whisking and as more oil becomes incorporated, speed up the drops into a thin, steady trickle. Once you have whisked in the sunflower oil, whisk in the olive oil in a still-thicker stream.

If you are using a food processor, do exactly the same thing, starting slowly then speeding up the oil addition as it is incorporated. Doing it in a machine gets a more 'set' mayo but be careful of it splitting at the early stage – the machine's blades need to be able to reach the purée and whisk it into the oil at the beginning. If the mayonnaise splits, put an egg yolk into a clean bowl and whisk it in drop by drop. The mayonnaise will come together again. Well done! Home-made mayo is the bomb!

THE BIG THREE

1. SULTRY, SMOKY CHIPOTLE

Add 1–3 tbsp Chipotles en Adobo (page 234) to the base for a smoky, spicy, rounded mayonnaise.

2. FLORAL, CITRUSSY HABANERO

Soak 3 habanero chillies in boiling water for 8 minutes to soften. Then blitz with the garlic and egg base with 1 tsp Mexican oregano and whisk in the oil as above.

3. GRASSY GREEN GARLICKY JALAPEÑO

Dry-roast 1–2 jalapeños or serranos in a hot dry frying pan (skillet) for 6–7 minutes until lightly charred all over. Blitz with the garlic and yolks. Lightly spiced, grassy green and garlicky, this is spectacular drizzled over almost anything, including the roast Sweet Potato Chunks on page 76, the Sweetcorn Nuggets on page 70 or the Summer Bean Tostadas on page 148.

HOME-MADE CREMA

For those of you who love experimenting with quirky recipes. Crema is somewhere between sour cream and crème fraîche in taste and is used in Mexico to garnish almost all savoury dishes, adding a subtle acidity to food or mellowing down bold flavours in chilli-spiked braises and salsas. It has a deliciously tangy flavour, a velvety texture and, like crème fraîche, can be used in hot food without it splitting. You will find yourself ladling it over all sorts of dishes. It transforms into the Spring Onion Crema (below) or pimp it by adding fresh herbs.

MAKES A SMALL BOWL

300ml (10½fl oz) double (heavy) cream

2½ tbsp buttermilk or plain yoghurt

pinch of salt

juice of ½ lime

Heat the cream in a pan to 35°C (95°F). Remove from the heat and pour into a sterilised jam jar or Kilner jar. Stir in the buttermilk and place the lid loosely on top, allowing some of the air in. Keep in a warm place for 24–36 hours and then refrigerate. Use as you would crème fraîche or sour cream. If it thickens too much, you can thin down with a tablespoon or two of cold milk.

Stored in an airtight container in the fridge, this will keep for 4–6 days.

CASHEW NUT 'CREMA'

We developed this dairy-free recipe for a supper club and it tastes great. It can be used throughout this book to add dairy-free velvety creaminess and a touch of acidity to your dishes, as you would use crème fraîche or sour cream.

MAKES A SMALL BOWL   (VO)

250g (9oz) raw cashews

40ml (1½fl oz) cider vinegar

40ml (1½fl oz) lime juice

1 tsp sea salt

Soak the nuts in 300ml (10½fl oz) water for 2 hours. Transfer them, with their water, to an upright blender, the more powerful the better. Blend the nuts on full speed, stopping a few times to stir and scrape the mixture down. After a minute, add the cider vinegar, lime juice and salt. Keep blending until all is smooth.

Stored in an airtight container in the fridge, this will keep for 4–6 days.

ALTERNATIVE

SPRING ONION CREMA

Blitz the griddled spring onions on page 238 with the crema above for a wonderfully creamy addition to a jacket potato or baked sweet potato. Or toss into a new potato salad with masses of fresh mint.

AVOCADO 'CREAM'

Barely a recipe but still worth noting as it is a brilliant vegan sauce, whose creaminess smooths out the flavours of fiery ceviches and other richly seasoned recipes. I use the coriander stalks as they have more flavour than the leaves and I hate wasting them. Quantities are approximate – adjust to taste!

MAKES A SMALL BOWL

1 large Hass avocado or 2 small

1½ tbsp lime juice (from 1–2 limes)

1½ tbsp chilled water

1½ tbsp extra-virgin olive oil

2–3 tbsp finely chopped coriander (cilantro) stalks

1 jalapeño or other green chilli, de-stemmed and roughly chopped (optional)

salt and pepper

Begin by deciding if you want the avocado cream spicy or not. If it is to accompany a spicy ceviche like the one on page 137, you could leave out the chilli. If you want to dollop it on the Quick-roast Cauliflower Taco like on page 94, add the chilli so that the 'cream' adds creaminess and spice.

Blitz the avocado flesh with the lime juice, chilled water and olive oil. Add 2 tablespoons of the chopped coriander stalks, 2–3 large pinches of salt and the chilli, if you are using. Blitz again to a smooth, thick cream. At this stage, taste and adjust the seasoning and consistency, both of which will depend on the size of your avocado and preference, with more salt, water, lime or oil.

Stored in an airtight container in the fridge, this will keep for a couple of days.

ALTERNATIVE

A DELICIOUS AVOCADO DRIZZLE

A fiery hot, thin version of this cream is popular in Mexico City taquerias – just keep adding enough chilled water to make the above recipe thin enough to drizzle and taste to see if you need to adjust the seasoning with a squeeze of lime or a pinch more salt and, indeed, more chilli, if you want it spicy.

HOW TOS

HOW TO HYDRATE CHILLIES

Tear out the stems from the chillies and discard the seeds. Flatten the chillies out like a book. Place a dry frying pan (skillet) over a medium–high heat. When medium-hot, gently toast the chillies for about 20–30 seconds each side. This gentle toasting brings out their flavour. They are ready when you can smell the oils, the skins start to soften and you can see them blistering in patches. Be careful not to burn them or they will lose their flavour and taste bitter.

Once toasted, pour just enough boiling water over to cover the chillies and weigh down, or if they have tougher skins like the chipotles, put in a small saucepan, cover with water and simmer gently for 15 minutes or until soft. Once soft, discard all but a few tablespoons of the soaking liquid and proceed with the recipe.

HOW TO DRY-ROAST INGREDIENTS FOR SALSA

Dry-roasting fruits and vegetables is a classic way to impart a smoky, robust flavour to salsas and sauces in Mexico, a cooking method practised for centuries and still used by modern chefs today. It is a simple technique to master. Simply place a large, heavy frying pan (skillet) over a high heat. Preferably use an old one as charring vegetables creates a mess. Char whole tomatoes; peeled onions, cut into fat wedges; whole tomatillos, soft husks peeled away; whole fresh chillies or unpeeled garlic cloves in the pan until blistered, blackened and softened all over. The garlic and chillies take 6–8 minutes (the garlic skins turn black but the cloves within soften when ready); onions, tomatillos and tomatoes take 10–15 minutes. Remove the garlic peel and the chilli stalks but everything else should be used, either smashed into a rough salsa in a pestle and mortar or whizzed in a blender to a purée.

HOW TO MAKE A GREAT FLOUR TORTILLA

It is so easy to make flour tortillas. No, I don't always have the time or the patience, but when I have one or the other it is a fun weekend escape and the results are mouthwateringly delicious. Kids love making these – it is pretty magical watching them puff up and blister.

MAKES 10–12 QUESTADILLA-SIZE OR 5–6 LARGER TLAYUDA-SIZE

250g (9oz) white spelt flour, plus extra for dusting

½ tsp baking powder

½ tsp salt

60g (2oz) butter, room temperature

190g (7oz) yoghurt

Combine the dry ingredients in a bowl and mix in the butter with your fingertips until you have a scruffy, scraggy dough. Add the yoghurt and knead for about 2–3 minutes in the bowl with your hands. Cover with a dish towel and rest for 30 minutes.

Lightly dust your work surface and divide the mixture into 50g (2oz) balls for large tacos or 80g (3oz) balls for tlayudas, covering them with a damp cloth as you do. Roll each one out on a floured surface, trying to make them as thin as you can, about 15cm (6 inches) for large tacos and approx. 20cm (8 inches) for tlayudas.

Place a non-stick pan (skillet) over a high heat and when properly hot, add a tortilla. Toast for about 30 seconds until it puffs up, then flip and cook for another 30 seconds on the other side. Put onto a hot plate with a dish towel over to keep them warm while you cook the rest.

HOW TO MAKE A GREAT VEGAN WHOLEWHEAT TORTILLA

Heritage wheats are all the rage, quite rightly. They can be grown in a way that sinks carbon back into the soil, they are much better for you and some of them taste amazing. Try adding stoneground wholemeal flour or a heritage wheat variety in place of some of the white spelt. You will really be able to taste the difference.

MAKES 10–12 QUESTADILLA-SIZE OR 5–6 LARGER TLAYUDA-SIZE

200g (7oz) white spelt flour, plus extra for dusting

100g (3½oz) stoneground wholemeal (wholewheat) flour, or other variety

½ tsp baking powder

½ tsp salt

50ml (2fl oz) vegetable oil

Use the instructions for the non-vegan tortilla opposite, adding 100ml (3½fl oz) of the water and the oil instead of the yoghurt and butter and adding more water if the dough needs it to come together. Rest for 30 minutes and proceed as the main tortilla recipe.

HOW TO MAKE TAMARIND PASTE

Break open the pods and submerge the fruit and seeds in just enough boiling water to cover. Help will be easy to enlist here – sucking on the fruit is as mouthwatering as sucking on a fizzy sour and my lot have been known to finish off half a box in one sitting. Leave for 5 minutes, then pop a pair of rubber gloves on and rub the fruity flesh from the seeds, dissolving it in the hot water.

Once the seeds are clean of the fruit, push the purée through a sieve into a small bowl. Your paste is now ready to use.

Stored in an airtight container in the fridge, this will keep for 4–5 days.

HOW TO MAKE A CORN TORTILLA

Whether eating at a table or on the go, you don't need a knife and fork to enjoy Mexican street food. Using the soft corn tortilla ('tor-tee-ya') as its base, street food originated with wives bringing farmers their midday meals using tortillas as wrapping. During the exodus from the countryside to cities, traders began offering this familiar 'home-cooked' food to newcomers. Stalls sprang up selling regional favourites from all the states of Mexico: Oaxaca, Michoacán, Sinaloa, the Yucatan, Veracruz and more, giving rise to perhaps the most diverse cuisine of all the Americas. These wraps are the real McCoy: soft, supple, bursting with flavour and so much better than anything out of an air-sealed packet!

SERVES 6 (VO)

400g (14oz) masa harina flour

½ tsp salt

300ml (10½fl oz) warm water

vegetable oil, for frying

You will need a clean plastic bag (preferably recycled), torn into its two halves, or two sheets of parchment paper and preferably a tortilla press, although you can get away with a rolling pin.

Combine the dry ingredients in a bowl, then gradually stir in the warm water until a dough begins to form. Knead in the bowl for 2–3 minutes until smooth, then cover with a dish towel and rest for 30 minutes. Pay attention to the texture – you want it to feel springy and firm, similar to the texture of play-doh. If the dough feels too wet and is sticking to your hands, add a few tablespoons of flour. If it feels too dry, add an extra tablespoon or two of warm water.

Divide into 30g (1oz) balls and place on a plate, covered with a damp cloth to stop them sticking. Put one half of the plastic or parchment onto the tortilla press or worktop and place your first ball in the middle. With two fingers, gently press down on the tortilla ball to squash it into a thickish disc. Cover with the second sheet of plastic, to stop the masa from tearing or sticking, and press or roll out into a thin tortilla, about 3mm (⅛inch) thick.

Peel away the top plastic, then pick up the sheet that the tortilla is on and flip it face down onto the opened palm of your hand, tortilla to skin. Peel away the plastic top and turn out the tortilla into a lightly oiled pan.

Cook on one side for 20–30 seconds, until the tortilla starts to look cooked, with lovely browned spots of toasting. If you are lucky it may even puff up! Turn and cook for another 30 seconds, then turn once more. Remove from the pan and keep wrapped up in a dish towel in a warm oven. Serve as soon as possible – there is nothing so bad as a cold tortilla, so the saying goes!

HOW TO MAKE A TOSTADA

A tostada is a crisp fried tortilla that, rather like a crispbread, provides the perfect base for a range of delicious Mexican toppings. They are a wonderful addition to a summery spread of Mexican tapas, otherwise known as *antojitos* in Mexico!

Frying stale tortillas, rather than fresh, will give you a crunchier tostada as they will absorb less oil.

Warm a couple of centimetres of oil in a frying pan (skillet) and individually fry small corn tortillas for approx. 30 seconds on each side until golden and crisp, then drain on kitchen paper.

Alternatively, dry-toast fresh tortillas in a dry frying pan until black in spots and brittle. Tostadas like these need to be served at once, or they will turn chewy.

I also make tostadas from pitta breads when I can't get hold of corn tortillas. Just use a ring cutter, cut out the size you want, brush with vegetable oil and bake in a 180°C/160°C fan/350°F/gas 4 oven for 4–5 minutes until golden and crisp.

HOW TO COOK DRIED BEANS (WITH & WITHOUT SOAKING)

A tin is fine when you are in a hurry, but there is something infinitely rewarding about cooking your own dried beans from scratch, plus you can start getting excited about buying exotic bean varieties from far-flung places.

Soaking dried beans overnight, covering with water and simmering until tender, yields delicious beans with the type of texture that makes you think of squashing a borlotti bean between thumb and finger on a hillside cantina in Tuscany. You never quite get that texture from a tin of beans. What about when you forget to soak them? Use this cheat's method – it works like a dream.

Cover the beans with cold water and bring to the boil. Simmer briskly for 10 minutes, then drain.

Now, cover the beans with cold water again with at least 8–10cm (3–4 inches) spare at the top. Add your seasonings (garlic, oregano, bay, epazote, hoja santa, anise, peppercorns) plus a scant teaspoon of bicarbonate of soda (baking soda). Bring to the boil again and cook as you would normally, not forgetting to skim off the white fluff on top of the beans.

Re-fry, put in a pot/casserole or purée as you see fit ....

HOW TOS

247

LOOKING FOR SOMETHING?

STOCKISTS

BEANS AND CHILLIES

Hodmedod's
hodmedods.co.uk

Chilli Pepper Pete
chillipepperpete.com

MEXICAN INGREDIENTS

Cool Chile Co
coolchile.co.uk

MexGrocer
mexgrocer.co.uk

SPECIALIST INGREDIENTS, TORTILLA PRESSES AND TEQUILAS

Sous Chef
soushchef.co.uk

Natoora
natoora.co.uk

Waitrose
waitrose.com

SPECIALITY SEEDS

Organic Catalogue
organiccatalogue.com

Ethical Organic Seeds
ethicalorganicseeds.co.uk

Sea Spring Seeds
seaspringseeds.co.uk

SEASONAL & LOCAL INGREDIENTS

Visit your local market, deli and grocer for locally grown, seasonal and fresh produce.

INDEX

ABOUT TOMMI

Cook, writer, TV and radio presenter, winner of *MasterChef* and mother of three, Tommi has made cheese and run market stalls in Ireland, cheffed with Skye Gyngell at Petersham Nurseries and in 2007, after living in Mexico for a year, co-founded Wahaca, winner of numerous awards for its food and sustainability credentials; in 2016 the whole restaurant group went carbon neutral. Tommi's passion lies in great food and how it can positively affect people and the environment: she co-founded the award-winning 'Pig Idea' campaign in 2015 with Tristram Stuart to tackle food waste, helped set up Chefs in Schools in 2017 for which she is a trustee, is an ambassador for the Soil Association and was awarded an OBE in 2019 for her services to the food industry. Tommi has a weekly column in the *Guardian's Feast* magazine, cooking simple but delicious seasonal recipes, regularly cooks at different events and shops at her local food market. *Meat-free Mexican* is her eighth cookery book after, among others, *Mexican Food Made Simple* and *Home Cook*.

ACKNOWLEDGEMENTS

I have always associated writing books with giving birth. (!) The experience is so intense that afterwards I tell myself that I will not jump so blindly into the next one. Amazingly, after *Home Cook* I paused and with three children, Wahaca and my column in the *Guardian* I had plenty to keep me busy. But after a while the lure of recipe creation proved too much. I find making a cookbook to be the most creative, exhilarating ride. Writing this one in the UK's bleak lockdown of early 2021 provided a welcome project and happy respite. Still, juggling family life, work life and writing life can be quite something and there is no way I could have made this book happen were it not a handful of amazing people. An enormous, HUGE thanks to you all.

Georgia Levy: For unflappable calm, unwavering loyalty and delicious kitchen artistry. Your help getting this book off the ground and support in recipe testing was invaluable.

El Kemp: What an intro! I had the most brilliant time cooking with you. Love your food, love your style.

Kitty Coles: The most creative, artistic foodie out there.

Evi O. Studio: For distilling my love of Mexico and its ingredients into this stunning book.

Tara Fisher: Is this our fifth book together???! For cherished memories of shoot days with you and your stunning pictures and to dancing in a field this summer.

Issy Gonzalez-Prendergast: For listening and listening, for gentle pressure and for constant encouragement.

To the teams at Wahaca, past and present, and in particular the food team with whom I have shared many a happy time in Mexico tasting the most delicious recipes and learning more about this most extraordinary cuisine: Carolyn Lum, Carlos Macias, Edson Diaz-Fuentes, Chris Buckley and Leo da Cruz – and to Mark Selby, my partner in Wahaca, for joining me on the ride.

My parents: To Dad, for building me the most epic kitchen to test my recipes, and the most amazing office to write them up in afterwards; to Ma, for just being the most loving and encouraging type of mother.

Mark W: For taking the children when I needed time and space to write. For an excellent critical appreciation of good food and for not being afraid to tell me when a recipe needed another go. For coping with me writing another book at a tricky time for you!

Also a huge thanks to my agents Holly Faulks and Antony Topping at Greene & Heaton; Georgia Rudd, Lucy Christian and Sophie Hoult for being my right hands; to Dodie & Jackson at Cool Chile Co. for providing chillies, corn, herbs and other exotic ingredients at the drop of a hat and for having set up in the first place so that there was actual supply of ingredients when we needed one; to Eduardo and Mex Grocer for appearing on my doorstep with hoja santa (best dried herb ever), achiote, dried hibiscus flowers, with cascabel chillies when I suddenly needed them in my kitchen for one particular recipe or another; to Scarlet & Violet for their stunning flowers and to the writers and cooks that have fuelled my imagination and inspired me: the one and only Skye Gyngell, Claire Thomson, Ed Smith, Margarita Carrillo, Enrique Olvera, Honey & Co, Nud Dudhia, Alice Waters, Diane Kennedy, Joseph Trivelli, Claire Ptak, Mark Diacono, Diana Henry, Yotam Ottolenghi, Gill Meller, Charles Dowding, Nigel Slater, Ravneet Gill, Gordon Ramsay, Alice Hart, Elena Reygadas and particularly Santiago Lastra who lent me a heap of his beautiful Mexican crockery for the shoot.

And to all the Mexican cooks who have spent time with me and shared ideas – thank you so much for your generosity and passion.

First published in Great Britain in 2022
by Hodder & Stoughton
An Hachette UK company

4

The authorised representative in the EEA is Hachette
Ireland, 8 Castlecourt
Centre, Dublin 15, D15 XTP3, Ireland (email: info@hbgi.ie)

A CIP catalogue record for this title is available
from the British Library

Hardback 9781529371840
eBook 9781529371857

Editor: Isabel Gonzalez-Prendergast
Design: Evi-O.Studio | Evi O., Susan Le
& Kait Polkinghorne
Photography: Tara Fisher
Food Stylist: Kitty Coles
Food Stylist Assistant: El Kemp
Props Stylist: Louie Waller
Production Manager: Claudette Morris

Colour origination by Alta London
Printed and bound in Germany by Mohn Media GmbH

Hodder & Stoughton policy is to use papers that
are natural, renewable and recyclable products and made
from wood grown in sustainable forests. The logging and
manufacturing processes are expected to conform to the
environmental regulations of the country of origin.

Hodder & Stoughton Ltd
Carmelite House
50 Victoria Embankment
London
EC4Y 0DZ
www.hodder.co.uk